JEWISH
CHOICES,
JEWISH
VOICES

POWER

The publication of this book was made possible
by a loving gift of
tikkun olam in memory of our parents,
Hannah and Harry Lensky and Sophia and Jacob Farb,
who taught us the meaning of taking care
of our fellow man.

Sylvia and Aubrey Farb

Support for this book is given in honor of our daughters,
Rachel and Zara Feingold,
in whom we see G-d's miracle every day.

Brenda Liebowitz and Aaron Feingold

JEWISH CHOICES, JEWISH VOICES

POWER

EDITED BY

ELLIOT N. DORFF

AND

LOUIS E. NEWMAN

2009 • 5769
Philadelphia

JPS is a nonprofit educational association and the oldest and foremost publisher of Judaica in English in North America. The mission of JPS is to enhance Jewish culture by promoting the dissemination of religious and secular works, in the United States and abroad, to all individuals and institutions interested in past and contemporary Jewish life.

The Jewish Publication Society
2100 Arch Street, 2nd floor
Philadelphia, PA 19103
www.jewishpub.org

Design and Composition by Progressive Information Technologies
Manufactured in the United States of America

09 10 11 12   10 9 8 7 6 5 4 3 2 1
ISBN: 978-0-8276-0862-7

Library of Congress Cataloging-in-Publication Data:
Jewish choices, Jewish voices / edited by Elliot N. Dorff, Louis E. Newman. — 1st ed.
　　v. cm.
　　Includes bibliographical references and index.
　　Contents: v. 1. The body
　　ISBN 978-0-8276-0860-3 (BODY)
　　ISBN 978-0-8276-0861-0 (MONEY)
　　ISBN 978-0-8276-0862-7 (POWER)
　　1. Jewish ethics.   2. Jews—Identity.   3. Body, Human—Religious aspects—Judaism.   I. Dorff, Elliot N.   II. Newman, Louis E.

　　BJ1285.2.J49 2008
　　296.3'6—dc22　　　　　　　　2007037402

JPS books are available at discounts for bulk purchases for reading groups, special sales, and fundraising purchases. Custom editions, including personalized covers, can be created in larger quantities for special needs. For more information, please contact us at marketing@jewishpub.org or at this address: 2100 Arch Street, Philadelphia, PA 19103.

CONTENTS

Acknowledgments

No series of books such as this comes about without the creative energy and support of many individuals. We wish to thank, first and foremost, Ellen Frankel, editor-in-chief of The Jewish Publication Society, for her vision in first conceiving of this series and her willingness to entrust it to our editorship. Her wise and patient guidance throughout the process of creating these volumes has been invaluable. The JPS National Council played a critical role early on as the scope and format of the series were in the development stage. Jane Shapiro's expertise as a Jewish educator was instrumental in helping us formulate the key issues around which to build each volume. Rabbis Aaron Alexander and Steven Edelman-Blank, both rabbinical students at the Ziegler School of Rabbinic Studies of the American Jewish University in the early stages of preparing the first three volumes of this series and now rabbis, collected, respectively, the classical and the contemporary Jewish sources for this volume. We are indebted to them for their fine work in locating these materials. The staff of The Jewish Publication Society has been a pleasure to work with at every stage of the production process. We wish to thank especially Carol Hupping, Lois Waitze, Janet Liss, and Michael Pomante for their professionalism, their responsiveness to all our requests, their patience with all our delays, and their persistent good counsel. Finally, we wish to acknowledge Peter Wieben, a student at Carleton College, for all his work in assembling the first three volumes of this series and preparing them for publication. His diligence and attention to detail are evident on every page of these books.

Description of the *Jewish Choices, Jewish Voices* Series

This series is intended to provide a forum for discussion of some of the most critical moral issues of our time. Although many of the topics chosen affect people of all ages, the series is designed to address particularly the moral problems faced by adults in their twenties and thirties.

Because the Jewish tradition is richly endowed with moral experience and insights, each volume of the series includes Jewish materials from ancient, medieval, and modern sources. And because the Jewish tradition, from its very beginnings, is multivocal, the sources presented deliberately include many Jewish perspectives from the past. The process of Jewish wrestling with moral subjects, however, continues on to our own day, and it does so not only theoretically but also concretely and practically. Each volume, therefore, presents cases that raise difficult, modern moral issues. We have also invited a number of modern Jews, representing a variety of backgrounds and Jewish perspectives, to comment either on those cases or on moral problems related to the book's topic that arise in their own lives, together with how they deal with them. This symposium both reflects on the meaning and application of the sources contained in the volume and extends the conversation into new areas of concern.

The introduction to each book describes the moral issues that the book raises and the Jewish investment in responding to them. The conclusion reflects back on the ground covered, including a broad look at the range of perspectives the book has documented and the meaning of those responses for future problems in the area of moral concern. In sum, then, the structure of each book is as follows:

> **Introduction:** The topic of the book, the range of moral issues that it raises, and its import for modern life and for Judaism
>
> I. **Case Studies and Jewish Sources:** Several cases illustrating some of the specific moral issues involved in the topic, including questions that highlight those issues, followed by ancient and modern Jewish sources relevant to those issues
>
> II. **Symposium:** Contemporary Jews' perspectives on the cases or on the book's topic as it emerges in their own lives

III. **Conclusion:** A summary of the underlying issues raised in the volume, together with some reflection on other related issues that may arise in the future

Our hope for this series is that Jews will be enriched both morally and Jewishly as they confront critical moral issues with the aid of classical and modern Jewish sources and multiple contemporary Jewish voices. Seeing moral issues through a Jewish lens, even one that produces multiple refractions of the Jewish tradition and of Jewish modernity, will, we hope, enable modern Jews to grapple with those issues more intelligently and more sensitively. It is our deepest conviction that these voices from the Jewish tradition and the Jewish community today will invite readers to consider their moral choices in a different light. At the very least, they give us all new questions and perspectives to ponder and, more often than not, moral wisdom and guidance.

Elliot N. Dorff
Louis E. Newman
July 2007

Introduction: Power

Forms of Power

"Power corrupts, and absolute power corrupts absolutely." Not so!—the Jewish tradition would say. Power is not in and of itself corrupting, any more than anything else in life is. It all depends on how those who have it use it.

The truth, though, is that historically Jews did not have very much power in the terms in which it is usually measured—namely, militarily and politically. Jews ruled themselves only three times during their history: from Moses (1250 B.C.E.) to the fall of the First Temple (586 B.C.E.) and with it the first Jewish commonwealth; the period of the Maccabees (165–64 B.C.E.); and finally in the modern state of Israel (1948 on). Even during those times, the Jewish state was anything but a world power.

If we look at the political influence of Jews, the picture is more mixed, for in some places and times Jews had considerable influence on the ruling powers. That is especially true in modern America, where, as of this writing, two of the nine Supreme Court justices are Jewish, the House of Representatives has some thirty Jewish members, and the Senate has thirteen, even though we constitute less than 2 percent of the U.S. population. That does not take into account all of the Jews who are now serving or who have served in government positions—from police officers on the street to cabinet secretaries.

If we mean economic power, the picture is even more mixed. Although the vast majority of Jews in most times and places were poor, some Jews at some times in history accumulated great wealth and enjoyed the power that came with those resources. Because Christian rulers during the Middle Ages and early modern period generally forbade Jews from owning farms and engaging in agriculture, which was considered honorable, Jews were forced to earn a living in trade and banking, both of which were considered morally shady. The result, though, is that Jews sometimes had money to lend to others. Non-Jews then often resented the power that Jews had, as depicted famously by Shakespeare's characterization of Shylock in *The Merchant of Venice.* As middle managers for Christian landowners, Jews were often the brunt of the anger of peasants, leading to many pogroms. Ultimately, anti-Semitic tracts, especially the *Protocols of the Elders of Zion,* depicted Jews as engaged in a worldwide conspiracy to rule the world. To this day, you sometimes hear, even in America, claims that Jews run the federal government, especially in regard to American policy toward the Middle East, as well as the world of entertainment and the media. Jews certainly play important roles in those arenas beyond what our numbers would suggest, but we are far from running either Washington or Hollywood. Jews are also involved in the businesses that they have created—sometimes very successful businesses, like Home Depot, Dell Computers, Ben and Jerry's, Victoria's Secret, and Seagrams—and are active in large, multinational corporations; but we have far less economic power than anti-Semites would lead people to believe. The vast majority of the wealth of America is still in the hands of Christians, and white Anglo-Saxon Protestant Christians at that.

Intellectual power is another matter. Here Jews have indeed excelled, both in times past and in contemporary times. Furthermore, the fields in which Jews have set the pace run the gamut from medicine and the biological sciences to the physical sciences, sociology and psychology (two fields largely created and populated by Jewish professionals), philosophy, political science, law, literature, music, art, drama, film, television, and technology. Jews constitute far more than 2 percent of the professorships in American universities, especially the most prestigious ones; and we have won Nobel Prizes far more than would ever be expected. The number of Jews in the legal and medical professions also goes beyond their percentage of the population, although the percentage of Jews in medical schools has recently declined appreciably. Even in the world of finance, still primarily the reserve of white Anglo-Saxon Protestants, Jews have taken increasingly significant roles in such fields as accounting and financial planning and management, including a U.S. secretary of the treasury.

Finally, if Judaism has done nothing else, it has given the world an immense reservoir of spiritual and moral power. Christians and Muslims, adherents of Judaism's two daughter religions, make up more than 50 percent of the world's people, and both of those religions are very much rooted in Jewish ideas and values, however much they have deviated from them. Jewish beliefs, practices, music, and familial and communal ties demonstrate a strength and wisdom born of thousands of years of experience, much of it under adverse circumstances, so that Judaism teaches us well what our priorities should be in life, especially because we cannot have everything. It also affords us a wealth of spiritual resources, including liturgy, psalms, proverbs, stories, and sermons, to be used in prayer and meditation as well as, perhaps uniquely, in a multitude of legal and theological materials to study and argue about. Furthermore, Judaism often serves as a very different lens—and often a wise and healthy corrective—to the predominant secular or Christian views of American society on moral topics—for example, civil rights, education, drug and alcohol abuse, sexual ethics, abortion, and stem cell research.

Jewish Attitudes toward Power

It is not only the historical record of Jewish power that has been mixed; the attitude of Jews and the Jewish tradition toward power has been mixed as well. On the one hand, there is an appreciation of power. The Torah, for example, describes God as *ish milhamah,* "a man of war" (Exodus 15:3), and later biblical books often describe God as *adonai tzeva'ot,* "the Lord of armies" (e.g., 1 Samuel 1:3,11, 4:4, 15:2), who gives Israel victory in battles and blesses them with nature's abundance (Leviticus 26:1–13; Deuteronomy 28:1–14) when they obey God's commandments but who will just as easily bring them defeat and natural disasters if they do not obey God's commandments (e.g., Leviticus 26:27–41; Deuteronomy 28:15–68). God serves in the Bible and in Rabbinic literature as a model for human beings. For example, God proclaims in the Torah, "You shall be holy, for I the Lord your God am holy" (Leviticus 19:2), and the Rabbis extend this modeling feature of God: "As God clothes the naked, you should clothe the naked . . . ; as God visited the sick, you should visit the sick . . . ; as God comforted mourners, so you should comfort mourners; as the Holy One buried the dead, you should bury the dead" (Babylonian Talmud, Sotah 14a). If God is portrayed as militarily powerful, then, presumably we should seek to be militarily powerful as well. Thus it is no surprise that David, who conquered Goliath and then expanded the Israelite kingdom to its widest borders, became a heroic figure in the Jewish tradition, whose descendant would usher in the Messianic Era through fighting a war against all the powers of evil (the "war of Gog and Magog") so that Messianic conditions of peace, prosperity, and justice could prevail (e.g., Isaiah 2:1–4; 11–12; Babylonian Talmud, Sanhedrin 97a–98a; Megillah 11a).

On the other hand, the tradition voices considerable concern about the use and abuse of power. In the Torah itself, Pharaoh is depicted as mean and stubborn, and the Song of the Sea (Exodus 15) celebrates God's victory over him. Even Israelite monarchs are viewed with suspicion. Samuel tries to convince the Israelites not to appoint kings in the first place but rather to continue to live under the authority of religious leaders; he only reluctantly succumbs to the will of the people to anoint a king when God specifically permits it (1 Samuel 8–10). The prophets strongly criticize many of the Israelite kings for their idolatry or adultery, including even David. Ultimately, the prophet Zechariah declares, "'Not by might, nor by power, but by My spirit'—said the Lord of Hosts" (Zechariah 4:6).

In the Second Temple period, a new form of leader arose, the sage, whose authority was based in his knowledge of the Torah rather than his military might. So worried were the sages about military leaders that they changed the Hanukkah story from one about human kings winning a war against the Seleucid Greeks and then rededicating the Temple, as reported in the book of Maccabees, to a story about the divine miracle of oil enough to last for only one day lasting eight (Babylonian Talmud, Shabbat 21b). The Rabbis also warn, "Love work, hate positions of domination; and do not make yourself known to the authorities" (Ethics of the Fathers 1:10) and "Be wary of the authorities! They do not befriend anyone unless it serves their own needs. They appear as a friend when it is to their advantage, but do not stand by a person in his hour of need" (Ethics of the Fathers 2:3). This wariness of military and political power, of course, is being voiced by people who fought the Romans and lost in Jerusalem (70 C.E.), at Masada (73 C.E.), and again at Betar (132–135 C.E.), so some of this may be the result of having been thwarted in their efforts to assert power militarily and politically. Still, the message of the Rabbinic tradition, followed by Jews until the rise of Zionism, is to appease the rulers and distance them as much as possible from the Jewish community. As the rabbi prays in the opening number of *Fiddler on the Roof,* "May the Lord bless and keep the czar—far away from us!"

Throughout the last two thousand years, though, Jews did exert and honor other kinds of power. Undoubtedly the most highly respected were the rabbis, those who knew the Jewish tradition and could explain and apply it to modern circumstances. The rabbis had not only spiritual power, bringing with it the power to persuade, but also legal power, with the power to enforce their rulings. Until the Enlightenment, Jews lived in communities in which most ruling powers demanded taxes from the Jews and sometimes men for the army but handed over day-to-day affairs to their own leaders, with the ultimate threat of enforcing those leaders' decrees on unruly members of the community. Thus Jews had courts at which rabbis presided; they had police; and they could punish wrong-doers with fines, lashes, and, ultimately, excommunication. This last punishment banned all members of the community from even talking to the person, let alone doing business with the wrongdoer, until he or she obeyed the decree of the court. All this changed when Jews became full citizens in the Enlightenment countries of western Europe and North America and thus began to use the government's courts for their own internal disputes as well as those with non-Jews; but because until the early twentieth century most of the world's Jews lived in eastern Europe or the eastern Mediterranean, where they were not full citizens, rabbis had juridical authority over them.

Even when rabbis had legal authority, there were clear limits on that authority. Some were imposed by the ruling power. So, for example, with the possible exception of eleventh- and twelfth-century Spain, rabbis did not have the authority to impose the death penalty. More important, the Talmud declares that the rabbis dare not decree something that the community cannot tolerate (Bava Kamma 79b; Bava Batra 60b; Avodah Zarah 36a; Horayot 3b). That is, the rabbis had to exercise some self-control on what they demanded of their communities. Still, they did have considerable legal authority for most of the last two thousand years. Modern rabbis no longer have that, given that almost all of the world's Jews live in countries governed by Enlightenment principles; but they do enjoy the persuasive power that comes with their position as the exponent of the Jewish tradition and, psychologically, as a parent figure.

Wealthy Jews also enjoyed prestige and power. From talmudic times they were known as *tovei ha-ir,* "the good men of the city" (Babylonian Talmud, Megillah 26a–b,27a), and they often functioned as aldermen. In that capacity, they could adopt ordinances to govern the community (*takkanot ha-kahal,* "decrees of the community"). That power brought with it, of course, the responsibility to provide for and guard the welfare of the community, including the poor; and such Jews were very much honored for functioning in this capacity. Knowledge of the Jewish tradition, however, was valued more than money. Thus Tevye in the Shalom Aleichem story that was put to music in *Fiddler on the Roof* dreams of being a rich man who can afford all the amenities and even the luxuries of life, including a staircase that goes to nowhere and a seat in the synagogue at the eastern wall (and thus closest to Jerusalem), but his ultimate dream is to know enough Torah so that he can ask a question that would cross a rabbi's eyes.

Knowledge of secular subjects, and particularly medicine, was also highly valued. As time went on, Jews in other professions—scientists, lawyers, accountants, artists, politicians—and in finance and business were also very much honored. As part of that respect, Jewish communities have come to call on these professionals when in need of their expertise, and so many have become active lay leaders of their Jewish communities.

Moral Issues Involved in Power

As the cases studies and essays presented in this volume illustrate, along with power comes not only responsibility but also moral ambiguity. On the social level, this is evident in the hard choices that Jewish agencies like Jewish Family Service must make in distributing its limited funds. In business, Jews involved in running corporations or other businesses must make some hard policy decisions affecting their employees, suppliers, and customers.

In Israel, of course, the social power of a sovereign state raises these issues even more sharply; Israel must contend with such issues as how to spend limited resources on competing social goods, how to rule a large minority, and how to preserve its moral integrity under conditions of continual warfare. Although the tradition bids us to seek peace, it is not pacifist and in fact demands that we defend ourselves from aggressors. This has led to a renewed respect for the military in Israel as well as some very deep thinking about the moral issues that military might entails. (*Note:* This volume does not treat the issues of war, which will be the focus of a future volume in this series.)

In the work environment, the moral issues of power include professional–client relationships and relationships among colleagues. Personal relationships also raise many issues of power, as, for example, in parent–child relations, dating patterns, and sexual relationships.

Ultimately, then, Jews need to confront the issues of power in both their personal and their professional lives. In doing so, it is important to remember that, as with money, the Jewish tradition does not assert that all power is bad but rather that the moral quality of power depends on how those who have it use it.

PART I

⚘

CASE STUDIES AND JEWISH SOURCES

First Case Study: Soliciting Charitable Donations

K AREN IS Jewish and a vice president of a large investment firm. She is heavily committed to a variety of charitable causes, and she knows that it would be good for her business to be known as a contributor to charity. She therefore wants to approach her subordinates to ask them for contributions to the following causes. Given the inequality in their power relationships, is it legitimate for Karen to ask the employees for contributions to any of these causes. If so, to which and why?

> *The local art museum*
> *The United Way*
> *The local Jewish Federation (assuming the employee is Jewish)*
> *Planned Parenthood*
> *The Republican Party*

Questions

1. Would it make any difference if Karen approached subordinates who were already giving to the cause in question and she was merely pressuring them to give more?

2. Would it matter if Karen pressured her employees to give money but left it to them to choose the recipients, provided that they inform her of their gifts so she could use the information in the corporation's public relations campaign?

Traditional Sources Relevant to All Cases

Compiled by Aaron Alexander

1. Genesis 3:22

And the Lord God said, "Now that man has become like one of us, knowing good and bad." [After Eve eats from the tree of knowledge of good and evil.]

2. Genesis 18:20–25

Then the Lord said, "The outrage of Sodom and Gomorrah is so great, and their sin so grave! I will go down to see whether they have acted altogether according to the outcry that has reached Me; if not, I will take note." The men went on from there to Sodom, while Abraham remained standing before the Lord. Abraham came forward and said,

"Will You sweep away the innocent along with the guilty? What if there should be fifty innocent within the city; will You then wipe out the place and not forgive it for the sake of the innocent fifty who are in it? Far be it from You to do such a thing, to bring death upon the innocent as well as the guilty, so that the innocent and the guilty fare alike. Far be it from You! Shall not the Judge of all the earth deal justly?"

3. Isaiah 1:17

Learn to do good.
Devote yourselves to justice;
Aid the wronged.
Uphold the rights of the orphan;
Defend the cause of the widow.

4. Mishnah, Avot, Ethics of the Fathers 1:14

This was another favorite teaching of his (Hillel):
If I am not for myself, who will be?
If I am for myself alone, what am I?
And if not now, when?

5. Mishnah, Avot, Ethics of the Fathers 2:1

Rabbi (Judah the Prince) taught:
Which is the path of virtue a person should follow?
That which brings honor to one's maker as well as respect from one's fellow human beings. . . .

Weigh the loss incurred in performing a commandment against the gain; conversely, weigh the gain of a sin against the loss.

Ponder three things and you will avoid committing a sin.
Keep in mind what is above you:
An Eye that sees, an Ear that hears,
A Book in which all your deeds are recorded.

6. Mishnah, Avot, Ethics of the Fathers 2:8

Another favorite teaching of his (Hillel):
More flesh, more worms; more possessions, more worries. . . .
However—more Torah, more life; more study with colleagues, more wisdom; more council, more understanding; more good deeds, more peace.

7. Mishnah, Avot, Ethics of the Fathers 3:16

Rabbi Yishmael taught: Be compliant with your seniors [superiors], be affable with your juniors, and greet every person with a cheerful manner.

8. Mishnah, Avot, Ethics of the Fathers 4:17

There are three crowns: the crown of Torah, the crown of Priesthood, and the crown of Royalty. The crown of a good name surpasses them all.

9. Babylonian Talmud, Shabbat 31a

Rava said: When one is brought [after death] for judgment, they ask: "Have you done business in good faith? Did you make time for study? Did you [engage] in procreation? Did you yearn for salvation? Did you delve deeply into wisdom? Did you discern one matter from another?" In any case: "Reverence for the Lord—that was his treasure" (Isaiah 33:6).

10. Babylonian Talmud, Sukkah 29b

Rav said: The property of householders may be confiscated [by the rabbinic court] for four reasons: (1) those who withhold wages of a hired hand; (2) those who oppress the hired hand; (3) those who take the yoke off of their necks and place it on their fellow's neck; (4) and those who are arrogant. But arrogance outweighs the others. And about humble people it is written: "But the lowly [humble] shall inherit the land and delight in abundant well-being" (Psalms 37:11).

11. Babylonian Talmud, Bava Metzi'a 10a

A worker may withdraw from his employment even in the middle of the day. For the children of Israel "are servants unto Me" (Leviticus 25:42). In effect, God says, "They are My servants, and not servants to other servants."

Traditional Sources for the First Case

Compiled by Aaron Alexander

1. Mishnah, Avot, Ethics of the Fathers 4:1

Who is honored? Those who honor all people; as it is written: "Those who honor Me, I will honor; but those who scorn Me will be despised."

2. Tanna de-Vei Eliyyahu Zuta 1

Whoever is able to perform an act of charity and does not, to save a person and does not, causes himself to perish.

3. Shocar Tov, Psalms 17

Even those who do evil but have acts of charity to their merit are worthy of and receive the Divine Presence.

4. Babylonian Talmud, Pesachim 50b

Rabba contrasted the following two verses: "For your faithfulness is as high as heaven . . ." (Psalms 57:11) and "For your faithfulness is higher than the heavens . . ." (Psalms 108:5). How are they different? The [second] refers to one who performs God's will for its own sake and the other [first] refers to one who performs God's will, but not for its own sake.

This is similar to what Rabbi Judah [taught], for Rabbi Judah said in the name of Rav: A person should always study Torah and perform good deeds, even though it is not for its own sake, for while doing so this person may come to do these actions for their own sake.

5. Babylonian Talmud, Sukkah 29b

Rabbi Yohanan said in the name of Rabbi Simeon ben Yohai [on the matter of why a stolen *lulav* is not valid for use on Sukkot]: It is [invalid] because [it is a case of] a commandment being performed through a sin.

6. Babylonian Talmud, Sotah 14a

Rabbi Hama, son of Rabbi Hanina, said: What is the meaning of the verse, "You shall walk behind the Lord your God" (Deuteronomy 13:5)? . . . [It means that] a person should imitate the righteous ways of the Holy One, blessed be God. Just as the Lord clothed the naked . . . so too you must supply clothes to the naked [poor]. Just as the Holy One, blessed be God, visited the sick . . . so too you should visit the sick. Just as the Holy One, blessed be God, buried the dead . . . so too you must bury the dead. Just as the Holy One, blessed be God, comforted mourners . . . so too you should comfort mourners.

7. Babylonian Talmud, Gittin 61a

We do not prevent poor non-Jews from collecting produce under the Laws of Gleaning, the Forgotten Sheaf, and the Corner of the Field [even though the Torah gives only poor Jews the right to collect these] for the sake of keeping peace.

Our Rabbis taught: We support the non-Jewish poor as well as the Jewish poor, we visit the non-Jewish sick as well as the Jewish sick, and we bury the non-Jewish dead as well as the Jewish dead for the sake of keeping peace.

8. Maimonides, Mishneh Torah, Laws of Gifts to the Poor 7:7

The Jewish and non-Jewish poor must be cared for in order to keep the peace.

9. Maimonides, Mishneh Torah, Laws of Gifts to the Poor 9:12

One who settles in a community for thirty days becomes obligated to contribute to the charity fund together with the other members of the community. One who settles there for three months becomes obligated to contribute to the soup kitchen. One who settles there for six months becomes obligated to contribute clothing with which the poor of the community can cover themselves. One who settles there for nine months becomes obligated to contribute to the burial fund for burying the community's poor and providing for all their needs of burial.

10. Maimonides, Mishneh Torah, Laws of Gifts to the Poor 10:7–8

7. There are eight levels of charity, one higher than the other. The highest merit in giving charity is attained by the person who comes to the aid of another in bad circumstances before he reaches the stage of actual poverty. Such aid may be in the form of a substantial gift presented in an honorable manner, or a loan, or the forming of a partnership with him for the transaction of some business enterprise, or assistance in obtaining some employment for him, so that he will not be forced to seek charity from his fellow men. Concerning this scripture says, "You shall strengthen him and he shall live with you" (Leviticus 25:35), that is, you shall assist him so that he does not fall.

8. The next lower level is giving aid to the poor such that the donor does not know to whom he has given and the poor person does not know from whom he has received. . . . Similar to this is one who gives to a charity fund, but one should not give to a charity fund unless one knows that those administering it are trustworthy and wise and know

how to administer it appropriately, like Rabbi Hananiah ben Teradyon [B. Bava Batra 10b].

Contemporary Sources for the First Case

Compiled by Steven Edelman-Blank

Source 1

WILLY: If I had forty dollars a week—that's all I'd need. Forty dollars, Howard.

HOWARD: Kid, I can't take blood from a stone, I—

WILLY, *desperation is on him now:* Howard, the year Al Smith was nominated, your father came to me and—

HOWARD, *starting to go off:* I've got to see some people, kid.

WILLY, *stopping him:* I'm talking about your father! There were promises made across this desk! You mustn't tell me you've got people to see—I put thirty-four years into this firm, Howard, and now I can't pay my insurance! You can't eat the orange and throw the peel away—a man is not a piece of fruit! *After a pause:* Now pay attention. Your father—in 1928! I had a big year. I averaged a hundred and seventy dollars a week in commissions.

HOWARD, *impatiently:* Now, Willy, you never averaged—

WILLY, *banging his hand on the desk:* I averaged a hundred and seventy dollars a week in the year of 1928! And your father came to me—or rather, I was in the office here—and he put his hand on my shoulder—

HOWARD, *getting up:* You'll have to excuse me, Willy, I gotta see some people. Pull yourself together. *Going out:* I'll be back in a little while.

> Arthur Miller, *Death of a Salesman: Certain Private Conversations in Two Acts and a Requiem* (New York: Penguin Books, 1976), 81–82.

Source 2

Tzedakah is all rage:
rage that people must run all over Creation
to gather every little spark from the First Light
God scattered in the worst places;
rage at Life's rules of some poor,
some smashed to inhumanly tiny pieces;
rage against the psychiatrists
who can't seem to tell us once and for all

why some people use their power, great or small,
to kick people around and kick them again when they are down;
rage that there is never enough money at the right moment
to save all wrongfully-dying infants in the world from death,
and that there are never enough
hours in a day
or days in a year
or years in a lifetime
to make some significant dent in the walls of human cruelty.
Cruelty is as hard as diamonds,
but Tzedakah should be the perfect blade
that cuts the ultimate exquisite facet
that makes the gems fit for human and Divine crowns.

> Danny Siegel, "Tzedakah Is All Rage," in *A Hearing Heart* (Pittsboro, NC: Town House Press, 1992), 24.

Source 3

Winter Sunday mornings in Detroit, my father and I would walk to the Warsaw Bakery on Twelfth Street to buy bagels. . . . No matter how early we came, the Pushke Lady was there before us, sitting in a chair safely out of the draft, shaking her canister under our noses. Jewish National Fund, Pioneer Women, Hadassah, milk for Jewish orphans, trees for Palestine—thanks to the Pushke Lady, no Jew would have to slather cream cheese on his bagel with a guilty conscience.

During the Depression, when we moved to a little town not far from Detroit, spring brought the tramps, pale and spindly, looking like plants do when they have had to reach too far to find the sun. Coming home from school, I would often spot a man at the back door looking for odd jobs, slouch hat or cotton cap held in both hands over his chest, hungry, and my mother would feed him: cold potatoes, bread, coffee; we had little enough ourselves. . . . Afterward, she would tell me, as though making excuses, "It's a *mitzvah* to feed the poor."

Our house was a regular stop for pious men in need of a kosher meal who might find themselves without time to reach Detroit or Chicago before sundown on a Friday night. . . . What has become of them, those grizzled men in long back coats, poring over yellowed prayer books by the light of our living room window on Shabbes mornings so long ago? My mother would believe they were in heaven now, saying prayers for all of us.

As a young married, locked into a small suburban community by babies and a lack of transportation, I met my fellow prisoners by collecting door to door for the Torch Drive, the name given to the United Way campaign in Michigan. In kitchen after kitchen, twin to my own, I drank coffee, shared recipes and surprising intimacies with barely post adolescent women like myself. Almost always, I came away with a few dollars in my envelope to justify my visit and the sense that I had performed a *mitzvah* to justify my life.

The children grew, and I collected: Dollars for Democrats, March of Dimes on Roosevelt's birthday, UNICEF on Halloween. Later, the Pushke syndrome became more complicated. When my oldest daughter was sixteen, I took her with me to the Alabama state capital to meet the Freedom Marchers who had walked from Selma to Montgomery. We both still remember the voice of Martin Luther King floating over our heads in the electric air and the long, sober train ride back with blinds drawn and lights out for fear of snipers. I didn't tell my daughter the trip was a *mitzvah* or that it was part of her *pushke* training, but she knows it now.

Living in Washington during the sixties, we made our home a way station for peace marchers. The spaghetti pot boiled, and the sleeping bags came out at the drop of a bullhorn. . . . I have met people, perfect strangers, who accurately describe the inside of our house and tell me they were drop-ins for this march or that. *They* may not realize they stand at the head of the symbolic queue that began for me with an old man who carried a prayer book in his satchel—but I do.

Faye Moskowitz, "The Pushke Lady," in *A Leak in the Heart* (Boston: David R. Godine, 1985); reprinted in *The Jewish Woman's Book of Wisdom: Thoughts from Prominent Jewish Women on Spirituality, Identity, Sisterhood, Family, and Faith*, ed. Ellen Jaffe-Gill (Secaucus, NJ: Birch Lane Press, 1998), 96–97.

Second Case Study: Developing Personal Relationships

Larry was ordained as a rabbi just last year. He has moved to his new congregation and has met a number of people his own age. He clearly wants to have friends in his new community, but Larry worries about the extent to which he can be friends with people who ultimately have the power to hire and fire him and who may at any time be consulting him on personal issues in his capacity as their rabbi.

Questions

1. To what extent may Larry seek out personal friendships with members of his congregation?

2. If Larry does make friends in the congregation, is it appropriate for him to expect that his new friends will order only kosher foods when they go out to eat?

3. Neil plays tennis with Larry each week, but was really bothered by Larry's disclosure that he enjoys surfing the Internet for adult pornography. Larry jokes that it does not hurt anyone and simply means that he is human, but Neil finds this behavior alarming. To what extent should Neil suppress his views altogether, convey them only in private and as a friend, or let the president of the congregation know about Larry's secret vice?

4. If Neil expresses his concern to Larry and Larry forbids him to tell anyone, should Neil do it anyway?

5. If Neil is a member of the committee negotiating an extension of Larry's contract, may he inform the committee of what he knows about Larry's private behavior? Given that Neil is a close friend of Larry's, should he absent himself from the contract committee altogether, irrespective of any knowledge he might have about Larry's private life?

Traditional Sources for the Second Case

Compiled by Aaron Alexander

(*Note:* For traditional sources relevant to all case studies, see p. 3.)

1. Exodus 18:17–22

But Moses' father-in-law said to him [when Moses acted as the only judge for all the Israelite people in the desert], "The thing you are doing is not right; you will surely wear yourself out, and these people as well. For the task is too heavy for you; you cannot do it alone.

Now listen to me. I will give you counsel, and God be with you! You represent the people before God: you bring the disputes before God, and enjoin upon them the laws and the teachings, and make known to them the way they are to go and the practices they are to follow. You shall also seek out from among all the people capable men who fear God, trustworthy men who spurn ill-gotten gain. Set these over them as chiefs of thousands, hundreds, fifties, and tens, and let them judge the people at all times. Have them bring every major dispute to you, but let them decide every minor dispute themselves. Make it easier on yourself by letting them share the burden with you.

2. Mishnah, Avot, Ethics of the Fathers 4:1

Ben Zoma taught:
Who is wise? Those who learn from everyone; as it is written: "From all my teachers have I gained understanding" (Psalm 119:99).

3. Mishnah, Avot, Ethics of the Fathers 4:9

Rabbi Yishmael, his (Rabbi Yose) son, taught:
A person who shuns the office of judge avoids enmity, theft, and perjury; but one who treats the judicial process lightly is a fool, wicked and arrogant.

4. Pesikta Rabbati, Piska 12

One is required to accord as much honor to disciples as to peers.

5. Babylonian Talmud, Berachot 17a

A pearl in the mouth of Abbaye: A person should always be subtle in finding ways to fear God. "A gentle response allays wrath; a harsh word provokes anger" (Proverbs 15:1). One should increase peace with his kinsmen, family and everyone, even with a non-Jew in the market, so that he may be loved above and cherished below and accepted by the people. They said that Rabban Yohanan ben Zakkai was never greeted first, even by a non-Jew in the market [for he would always be the first to extend his greeting].

6. Babylonian Talmud, Pesachim 87b

Rabbi Yohanan said: Woe to those who have great authority, for it buries those who possess it.

7. Babylonian Talmud, Ta'anit 7a

Rabbi Hanina said: I have learned much from my teachers, more from my colleagues, and from my students more than them all.

8. Babylonian Talmud, Sanhedrin 88b

One who is wise, modest, and fears sin, whose age is proper, and whom people find pleasant—is made a judge in his city.

9. Maimonides, Mishneh Torah, Laws of Ethics (De'ot) 5:2

When a wise person eats the small amount appropriate for him, he should only eat it in his house and on his table. [He should] not eat it in a store or in a market, unless there is a great need, lest he be viewed by others as without respect. [He should also] not eat with the non-learned. . . . .

It is only appropriate for him to eat with others at an obligatory feast, for example, an engagement or wedding feast. And this is only when the child of a wise person marries the child of another wise person.

10. Maimonides, Mishneh Torah, Laws of Ethics (De'ot) 5:7

A sage should not shout or shriek while conversing like cattle or wild beasts, nor should he lift his voice too much; rather, he should speak gently with all people. Also, he should be careful not to create too much distance while conversing, lest he appear arrogant. He should greet all people before they greet him so that they will feel good about him. He should give everyone the benefit of the doubt, speak favorably of his fellow, not degrade him [his fellow] in any way, and love peace and pursue peace.

11. Maimonides, Mishneh Torah, Laws of Ethics (De'ot) 6:1

A person's natural inclination is to follow the character and deeds of his friends and neighbors, and to act in accordance with local custom. Therefore, one needs to constantly associate with righteous people and dwell among wise people because much can be learned from them. On the other hand, one should distance oneself from wicked people who walk in darkness so that he will not be influenced by their actions.

12. Maimonides, Mishneh Torah, Laws of Ethics (De'ot) 6:3

Each person is commanded to love fellow Jews as they love themselves, as it is written, "Love your fellow as yourself" (Leviticus 19:18).

Therefore, one should speak praise about others and be concerned for their money—just as one would [be concerned] about one's own money and honor.

Contemporary Sources for the Second Case

Compiled by Steven Edelman-Blank

Source 1

In a rabbi, a great capacity for friendship is vital. This does not imply descending to the lowest denominator of hilarity, or rolling up one's sleeves to become one of the gang. It does imply the capacity to trust and to be trusted.

> Alfred Gottschalk, *To Learn and to Teach: Your Life as a Rabbi*, rev. Gary P. Zola (New York: Rosen Publishing Group, 1988), 52.

Source 2

A rabbi is a symbolic exemplar of the best that is in human kind. This is an essential inescapable component of the rabbinate. Being a living symbol is both the glory of a rabbi's life and a torment of a rabbi's inner being. The awesome ambiguities of rabbinic symbolic exemplarhood make the inner life of a rabbi extraordinarily vulnerable. For life as a pulpit rabbi to be viable, a rabbi must clean up some of the debris in one's inner life, make some order, and engender a greater sense of inner balance.

The awesome ambiguities are that, though "only" human, each rabbi is a Symbolic Exemplar of the divine *and* of a people who encountered the divine. Vertically, rabbis are Symbolic Exemplars of God and are expected to emulate and "stand in" for God. Horizontally, rabbis are Symbolic Exemplars of the Jewish people, enjoined to love and care for every last one. External courage and inner fortitude are demanded in living daily in the world as Symbolic Exemplars and moving forward in that world, with all one's frailties, deficiencies, inadequacies, and wounded "*selves*." The stress and strain of being Symbolic Exemplars, and its weight on their inner life, rabbis know from their everyday "being" in the rabbinate.

> Jack H. Bloom, *The Rabbi as Symbolic Exemplar: By the Power Vested in Me: For Rabbis, Other Clergy, and the Laity Who Care about Them and Their Sacred Work* (New York: Haworth Press, 2002), 153.

Source 3

Although human beings have always been susceptible to distorting interpersonal relationships by perceiving people differently than they are, it was not until the twentieth century that this process was named and systematically explored: The concept of transference, which was among Sigmund Freud's most significant contributions to our understanding of human psychology, refers to the fact that human beings are not capable of entering a new relationship as completely new. Instead, perceptions and experiences of people in the present are colored by experiences with people in the past and by recent or even current environmental influences and relationships. . . . Transference that perceives the rabbi as larger than life, capable of constant availability, and wise and loving at all times is based on a mixture of nostalgic fantasy, a wish for perfect superparent, and a hope for the rabbi to be the unifier of a community at an historical moment when liberal Jewish communities, with all their diversities, have no unifying practice. As the symbol of Jewish tradition and continuity, the rabbi is expected to be all things to all people and to be a kind of superglue capable of holding everything and everyone in a community together.

Barbara Eve Breitman, "Foundations of Jewish Pastoral Care: Skills and Techniques," in *Jewish Pastoral Care: A Practical Handbook from Traditional and Contemporary Sources*, ed. Dayle A. Friedman (Woodstock, VT: Jewish Lights Publishing, 2001), 94–96.

Source 4

In addition to their roles as teachers of Torah, rabbis are professionals who also play pivotal roles in bringing Jewish values to their communities. It is not sufficient to *talk* about the importance of justice and caring, respectful listening and welcoming, honesty and openness. Jewish communities must embody the values they espouse if they are to be taken seriously and if they are to serve as places where Jews can sanctify their lives. In the course of their training, Reconstructionist rabbis are therefore taught the skills that enable them to inspire and strengthen such caring communities.

Rebecca T. Alpert and Jacob J. Staub, *Exploring Judaism: A Reconstructionist Approach* (Elkins Park, PA: Reconstructionist Press, 2000), 154.

Third Case Study: Monitoring Ethics in Business

Olivia is the executive secretary to Peter, who is the vice president of an Internet company. She has worked in her current position for two previous vice presidents, and she understands what her boss's job entails. Olivia loves working for Peter because he is both kind and talented. However, she discovers that he has done one of the following things:

1. Peter has taken money from one budget and used it to pay expenses related to another budget because he wants one segment of the business to look more efficient than it really is.

2. Peter has taken money from the company and used it to pay for personal expenses, such as uncovered medical costs for a sick child.

3. Peter has begun to flirt with Ruth, another employee of the company, and Olivia has overheard Peter promise Ruth a raise if she has sex with him.

4. Peter continually neglects to make deadlines for budget reports and wrongly blames others for the delays.

5. Peter's actions show that he does not really know how to do his job.

Question

What should Olivia's reaction be in each case? For example, she could do any of the following:

a. Say nothing.

b. Talk directly to Peter.

c. Write a memo to Peter so there is a paper trail about this issue, which could protect her in case there is a lawsuit.

d. Lodge a formal complaint to the president of the company.

e. Quit her job.

Traditional Sources for the Third Case

Compiled by Aaron Alexander

(*Note:* For traditional sources relevant to all case studies, see p. 3.)

On Deception and Fraud
1. Exodus 23:7

Keep far from a false charge.

16

2. Leviticus 19:11

You shall not steal; you shall not deal deceitfully or falsely with one another.

3. Tosefta, Bava Kamma 7:8

Stealing a person's mind [*genevat da'at,* i.e., deception] is the worst form of theft.

4. Babylonian Talmud, Hullin 94a

We are taught on early rabbinic authority that a person should not sell anyone shoes made from the hide of an animal that died by itself, and claim the animal was actually slaughtered, for two reasons: First, because the seller is deceiving the buyer. Second, there is an element of danger involved [for the animal may have died from a disease that could endanger the buyer of the shoes].

5. Mishnah, Bava Metzi'a 3:3

Just as the law against fraud applies to buying and selling, so too does it apply to spoken words. One should not say, "How much does this product cost?" without wishing to purchase it.

On Rebuking a Wrongdoer
6. Leviticus 19:17

Reprove your kinsman but incur no guilt because of him.

7. Proverbs 9:7–9

To correct a scoffer,
Or rebuke a wicked man for his blemish,
Is to call down abuse on oneself.
Do not rebuke a scoffer, for he will hate you;
Reprove a wise man, and he will love you.
Instruct a wise man, and he will grow wiser;
Teach a righteous man, and he will gain in learning.

8. Tanhuma, Mishpatim 7

How do we know that one who observes an individual doing something improper is obligated to reprove him? The Torah teaches, "Reprove your kinsman . . ." (Leviticus 19:17). If one reproves and the other does not accept it, how do we know that one must again reprove him?

The Torah teaches, "Reprove [in the emphatic form of the Hebrew, using both the infinitive and finite form of the verb]" (Leviticus 19:17). Is this so even if one embarrasses the person? [No, for] the Torah teaches, "but incur no guilt because of him" (Leviticus 19:17). I know this [that we must reprove those who do something wrong] only with regard to a teacher [reproving a student]; how do I know that it applies also for a student to a teacher? The Torah teaches, "Reprove" [in the emphatic form, which implies] in every instance. And one who does not reprove bears responsibility for that transgression. As it has been said, anyone who can protest [the misdeeds of] one's household but does not do so is held accountable for the [misdeeds of the] household; likewise, with respect to [the misdeeds of] those in one's own town; likewise, with respect to [the misdeeds of] the whole world.

9. Babylonian Talmud, Shabbat 54b–55a

Rabbi Zera said to Rabbi Shimon, "Go, sir, and rebuke the members of the Exilarch's household." "They will not accept it from me," he replied. "Though they may not accept it, rebuke them anyway, sir," he answered.

10. Tosafot to the Babylonian Talmud, Shabbat 54b–55a

"Though they may not accept it"—in this case it is uncertain as to whether or not [the rebuke] will be accepted . . . but in a case where it is certain that it will not be accepted, it is better that they sin through ignorance than presumption.

11. Babylonian Talmud, Arakhin 16b

How far must one go in rebuking another? Rav said, "Until cursed." Shmuel said, "Until struck."

12. Mishnah, Avot, Ethics of the Fathers 1:7

Nitai, of Arbel, taught:
Keep far from an evil neighbor;
Be not a partner with an evil person;
Never despair retribution for the wicked.

13. Maimonides, Mishneh Torah, Laws of the Foundations of the Torah 6:7–8

If one observes that a person committed a sin or walks in a way that is not good, it is a duty to bring the erring man back to the right path and point out to him that he is wronging himself by his evil course, as it is said, "You shall surely rebuke your neighbor" (Leviticus 19:17). He who rebukes another, whether for offenses against the rebuker himself or for sins against God, should administer the rebuke in private, speak to the offender gently and tenderly, and point out that he is only speaking for the wrongdoer's own good, to secure for him life in the world to come. If the latter accepts the rebuke, well and good. If not, he should be rebuked a second, and a third time. And so one is bound to continue the admonitions until the sinner assaults the admonisher and says to him, "I refuse to listen." Whoever is in a position to prevent wrongdoing and does not do so is responsible for the iniquity of all the wrongdoers whom he might have restrained.

14. Maimonides, Mishneh Torah, Laws of Ethics (De'ot) 6:1

A person's natural inclination is to follow the character and deeds of his friends and neighbors, and to act in accordance with local custom. Therefore, one needs to constantly associate with righteous people and dwell among wise people—because much can be learned from them. On the other hand, one should distance oneself from wicked people who walk in darkness so that he will not be influenced by their actions.

15. Maimonides, Mishneh Torah, Laws of Ethics (De'ot) 6:3

Each person is commanded to love fellow Jews as they love themselves, as it is written, "Love your fellow as yourself" (Leviticus 19:18). Therefore, one should speak praise about others and be concerned for their money—just as one would [be concerned] about his own money and honor.

16. Maimonides, Mishneh Torah, Laws of Ethics (De'ot) 6:7

One who sees his fellow sin or stray down an improper path, it is an obligation (*mitzvah*) to correct his behavior [or attempt to] and tell him that he is sinning against himself with these bad deeds, as it is written, "Reprove your kinsman" (Leviticus 19:17). A person who rebukes his fellow, due to a deed done against him or someone else, or against God, should do so privately. He should speak to him gently and with a soft voice, and let him know he is telling him only for his own good.

17. Tanna de-Vei Eliyyahu Zuta 1

Whosoever is able to perform an act of charity and does not, to save a person and does not, causes himself to perish.

Contemporary Sources for the Third Case

Compiled by Steven Edelman-Blank

Source 1

We spend a lot of time trying to uncover people. Newspapers disclose facts about the private lives of public figures. Gossip columns strip them bare. We go into therapy and dissect our loved ones to pieces. We pick our friends apart behind their backs. We watch talk shows that encourage people to bare their souls to millions of onlookers. We want to know.

There are certain situations when it is crucial to reveal the truth about someone. But is there no room for shelter?

Most children learn about Noah in Sunday school. He is the man who built the ark and filled it with the animals two by two. But most of us never learned about what happened to Noah after the flood. Noah plants a vineyard, gets drunk, and exposes himself. His youngest son walks in on his father in his state of shame and runs to spread the news to his older brothers. But the brothers walk into their father's tent backward and avert their eyes so as not to look upon their father in his nakedness. They spread out a cloak and cover him up in compassion and respect.

What would happen if, instead of trying to expose people, we tried to cover them up? What if, instead of searching for their flaws, we tried to overlook their shortcomings? What if we were to embrace our loved ones with all their faults and imperfections? What if we refused to listen to reports that invade people's privacy? Our world desperately needs an infusion of compassion. We pray that God will shelter us and not judge us too harshly. Can't we learn to offer this same kindness to each other?

> Naomi Levy, "Shelter," in *Talking to God: Personal Prayers for Times of Joy, Sadness, Struggle, and Celebration* (New York: Doubleday, 2003), 242–43.

Source 2

There is truth and then again there is truth. For all that the world is full of people who go around believing they've got you or your neighbor figured out, there really is no bottom to what is not known. The truth about us is endless. As are the lies.

Philip Roth, *The Human Stain* (New York: Vintage International, 2000), 315.

Source 3

The guiding principle for disseminating negative information is when the information's recipient will suffer from a "clear and present danger"— not necessarily a life-threatening one—if he or she doesn't possess these facts.

Joseph Telushkin, *Words That Hurt, Words That Heal: How to Choose Words Wisely and Well* (New York: William Morrow, 1996), 49.

Source 4

A whistle-blower is a bystander who valiantly decides to give up his or her post of indifference, abandoning the security that comes with anonymity. As Wigand came to learn, resisting the temptation to remain spineless and willfully unaware requires extreme self-sacrifice, a burning sense of morality, and a willingness to face danger. Such charitable acts were rare during the Third Reich, where the presence of smoking chimneys was more lethal and grotesque than a mere cigarette. But even in cases where corporations serve shareholders over citizens and where professional ethics are hostage to a rising stock market, the moral imperative for the Wigands of the world to come forward is equally great, and in many ways, far less threatening. Today, with corporate mergers compressing the scope of collective interests, subverting the free flow of information, and creating such vast spectacles of wealth, how much harder will it be for those willing to blow the whistle to do so while standing inside the otherwise sound-proof corridors of corporate greed?

It is ultimately a job for someone with healthy lungs, because it invariably requires the summoning of the troops. The person must be a primal screamer: the rebel yell clears the conscience. Given the extreme demands on the breath, however, such a person probably shouldn't take up smoking. Yet, maybe it would be better if such displays of courage were themselves habit-forming, so the rest of us could get hooked on something that is so generous to the spirit and unhazardous to everyone's health.

Thane Rosenbaum, "'Smoked Out,' Review of *The Insider* (Touchstone Pictures)," *Tikkun*, 15, no. 2 (March/April 2000), 79–80. [The film

The Insider tells the story of tobacco-industry whistle-blower Dr. Jeffrey Wigand.]

Source 5

LARRY KING, HOST: Tonight, a prime-time exclusive. Bob Woodward and Carl Bernstein, the reporters who broke the Watergate story that brought down a presidency, in their first live prime-time interview since they got scooped by their legendary source, Deep Throat [named Mark Felt], when he suddenly revealed the identity they'd kept all secret for 30 years. . . .

CARL BERNSTEIN, WASHINGTON POST: . . . The country was served because here was a man who told the truth while the President of the United States and the Justice Department and the apparatus of the government were engaged in massive corruption and would not tell the truth about the most serious constitutional crimes in our history. . . .

WOODWARD [Bob Woodward, *Washington Post*]: . . . He is a man who's 91 now, cared for lovingly by his family, by his daughter, Joan, whom I got to know some over the years, who's interested in his welfare. She believed he was Deep Throat. This is a man, during Watergate and during the years since Watergate, [who] was in turmoil, profound ambivalence about what he had done, whether he had broken the code within the FBI, or whether he had done something that was absolutely necessary to explain that there was this massive law-breaking and obstruction of justice going on, led by, as we now know from the tapes, the President himself. So he found his duty, but never, I think, felt totally comfortable with it.

> *Larry King Live* [CNN], June 2, 2005. LexisNexis Academic search conducted August 2, 2005.

Source 6

Now, we read that Mark Felt's family and Mark Felt put out their story solely to make money off it. So, this makes the family's karma even more unnerving. The father, patriarch, Mark, took out his anger and frustration for being passed over at the FBI, by ruining the career of the peacemaker, Richard Nixon. So, he condemned a whole subcontinent to genocide and slavery and poverty to please his own wounded vanity. (Maybe his nickname should be "sour grapes" and not "deep throat" because he has as much in common with that fox as with a porn star.) And, blood will tell, as the old saying goes: his posterity is now dragging out his old body and putting it on display to make money. (Have you noticed how Mark Felt looks like one of those old Nazi war criminals they find in Bolivia or Paraguay? That same, haunted, hunted look combined with a glee at what he has managed to get away with so far?)

Ben Stein, "I Don't Feel for Felt," *American Spectator,* June 3, 2005, available at www.spectator.org/dsp_article.asp?art_id=8255. [In the next paragraph, Stein mentions that Felt may be partially Jewish. As far as we can find, he is not.]

PART II

❧

SYMPOSIUM

The Power of Executives

A Respectable Business Plan: Managing a Company the Jewish Way

Aaron Feuerstein

TO MANAGE the American enterprise system ethically requires that we remunerate all our workers with a living wage. That means that the wages must be at least above the poverty level and that labor be treated as human beings who are created in the image of God.

Since wages are determined by the availability of labor at a given skill level—the law of supply and demand—whenever that labor is transplantable and more costly in the United States than in other parts of the world, such as China and India at under $1 an hour, outsourcing is employed, which results in wages below the poverty level.

Giving to charity at the end of a profitable year or at the end of a lifetime of profits is laudatory but cannot make up for paying poverty wages or for having unethical relations with workers. Charity giving can benefit humankind and the world immeasurably but cannot compensate for treating workers as objects—as a pair of hands.

The ethical foundation on which our country and Western civilization is built is, in the last analysis, derived from the Hebrew Bible, Leviticus 19:18: "Love your fellow as yourself," or as Hillel said, "That which you find intolerable, do not do to your neighbor." For the CEO, that means to consider the worker a stakeholder just as the CEO is a stakeholder.

The exaltation in the United States of our human and social values has no meaning if it excludes our workers. Our democracy can find its greatness not on how much money it makes but on the humane system it uses in creating that money. Our superpower leadership will become permanent not from its immensity but from the quality of its human and social values.

There is a beautiful narrative recorded in the Talmud concerning the controversies and legal discussions between two of our leading scholars, Hillel and Shammai, that occurred approximately 2,000 years ago. The town fool entered the academy of learning and demanded to be told the defining message of the Jewish religion in the short space of time during which he had the strength to stand on one foot. Considering it impossible to define the complexities of the laws and commandments of the Torah in the time afforded, Shammai refused. Then Hillel interjected. "Leave him alone! Yes we can explain the Jewish religion in less than even a minute: 'Love your neighbor as yourself'" (Leviticus 19:18). That is the essence of the Jewish religion and the Torah. Everything else is derived from that.

When I was a youngster, our family would eat dinner together every night. To this day, I still consider it an honor to have been present with my parents and my siblings at my father's table. We would discuss everything—school, religion, politics, and so on. It was wonderful. I recall when I was a kid my father, Samuel C. Feuerstein, spoke of how, when he was 14 years old, he started working for his father, Henry Feuerstein, in the Malden Knitting Mills, which was incorporated in 1906. He observed that my grandfather, who started the business, would go around the mill every evening at about sunset when the workday was over and pay each and every worker the wages due to him. My father suggested to my grandfather that this custom was not done here in the United States; instead, what should be instituted was a record-keeping system that tallies the wages, hours, benefits, and taxes on a weekly basis while actual payment would be made in arrears the following week. In response, my grandfather cried out, "No! It's against the Torah, it's against the Bible!"

The very next day after hearing this story and after public school in Brookline, Massachusetts, I had my daily Hebrew lessons with my maternal grandfather, Rabbi Raphael Landau. I related to him everything that transpired between my father and my grandfather and asked, "How is it possible that the Bible would be in opposition to paying in arrears?" He answered, "Yes, your grandfather is right. It's in the Torah." He showed me Deuteronomy 24:14–15, which I committed to memory. "You shall not abuse a needy and destitute laborer, whether a fellow countryman or a stranger in one of the communities of your land. You must pay him his wages on the same day, before the sun sets, for he is needy and urgently depends on it." Workers ought to be treated as human beings who are created in the image of God. The workers render their services as human participants in the enterprise, not as pairs of hands. They have souls that should be respected. And I firmly believe, as a result of my own experience, that this respect becomes mutual so that in the long run the enterprise will benefit over and above the cost involved. As a case in point, during and after a devastating fire at our mill on December 11, 1995, we were able to recover rapidly and continue business as a result of the sacrifice and dedication of our loyal workers way above any call for duty.

To ensure that our corporation would act ethically, we created a mission statement for Malden Mills; the result of the best thinking of our top management, the statement provides all our employees with reasonable guidelines within which to operate. This is our mission statement: "We are dedicated to providing the most technically advanced and best-known textiles and related products through continuous innovation, outstanding quality, creative brand marketing, and excellent customer service from a caring, ethical, safe, and environmentally responsible corporation that benefits all of its partners (employees, customers, shareholders, suppliers, lenders, and the community)."

Our mission statement promotes profitability by championing a forward-looking business strategy and simultaneously insisting that it must be accomplished ethically. What we are saying here at Malden Mills is that it is incumbent upon the business and its top management to merge these two objectives—business profits and social responsibility—and to do it in a reasonable way. A proper balance is what the CEO should strive for in the management of the company.

Unfortunately, many CEOs today would claim that completely maximizing the profitability to the shareholder is the only objective and that it has nothing to do with ethics and sensitivity to the human equation. They might add that they're not opposed to ethics and charity—that's fine on Christmas Day and the Day of Atonement when you go to church or synagogue. Those are the times for values; but merging them with the management of a business creates a contradiction.

In my judgment, if you consider increasing the profitability to the shareholder only in the short term, then traditional CEOs might have a point. However, I think of profitability to the shareholders in the long term; and I am confident that, in the long run, profitability will be increased if management is sensitive to the welfare of the workers.

Furthermore, I am confident that our business strategy, as stated in Malden Mills's mission statement, is economically justifiable. Any company can have a mission such as ours and, at the same time, be profitable without concentrating exclusively on labor cost. There are three parts to this type of success: *quality*, *brand*, and *research and development*.

Quality

Malden Mills is dedicated to producing the very best quality products we can make. We do not stop until that quality is truly the best in the world. We differentiate ourselves from the global commodity market, which does not have the same kind of quality but fights for business on the basis of price. The country that has the cheapest labor has the best price and wins that ball game. We are not involved in that rat race. We distance ourselves from it. We insist on the best quality. In the last analysis, that is really what we have to sell. What better way could there be to secure that quality than by being sensitive to the needs of the workers who, in fact, are the very ones who are *making* that quality? *It is their morale and determination* that give us the best quality. When, at the time of the fire on December 11, 1995, I said that the workers are our greatest asset, I meant it.

Brand

We commit our human and financial resources to branding the best quality. Malden Mills has worked out a brand that is an ingredient brand because our product—fabric—is not the final product the consumer buys. It is part of the final product produced by our customers, such as Patagonia, North Face, and Arc'teryx; therefore, we call it an "ingredient." We want the retail customer to know that the item he or she is buying from one of our direct customers is made of our product and it is the best.

Research and Development

At Malden Mills, we commit our financial and human resources to research and development and innovation. We think it is critical that a brand not live solely on its past history but that innovations are introduced so rapidly that one's own products become obsolete; this is seen especially in today's electronic and high-technology fields. We expect to do exactly the same thing with our product so that which is copied offshore will be obsolete.

The three-part strategy of quality, brand, and research and development can be accomplished even when adhering to a mission statement such as ours. There's no need to wring every last cent out of labor.

The plan that we have improves the manufacturing base of the United States and gives a self-respecting livable wage to the workers so they can be responsible for a family and see that their children can be educated. When a worker loses a manufacturing job to off-shoring, the employment figures may show that he or she was able to find another job; unfortunately the new job is often in the service industry at or close to minimum wage, which provides an income that is below the poverty level. What is happening is the substitution of a self-respecting wage for one that breeds despair. The unconscionable spread between the entrepreneurs—those who are marketers, financial wizards, or innovators—and the working class gets bigger. The difference between the CEOs' wages and the wages of the workers keeps growing. If we continue with this trend of removing the manufacturing base from the United States, the wage spread will only get worse. To the extent that our working class is unable to sustain itself and loses its vitality, we could ultimately lose our democratic institutions and security. Our democracy depends on a strong, vibrant, and hopeful middle class and working class, the weakening of which could very well bring about the loss of that democracy.

Outsourcing could be beneficial to our country as long as it is planned carefully so as not to upset the balance among the entrepreneurs, the middle class, and the working class. If outsourcing is left entirely to the greed of many of our CEOs, boards of directors, and Wall Street without suitable government parameters within which to operate, we could very well lose our country. All our creativity should go into developing legislative parameters to protect our workers and at the same time not interfere with the profitability of our economy.

To paraphrase Micah's monumental pronouncement:

He has told you, O CEO, what is good,
And what the Lord requires of you:
Only to operate your business justly
And pursue employee loyalty with compassion,
And to walk humbly with your God-derived ethical values (Micah 6:8).

"You're No Sammy Glick": Ethics and Power in a Cutthroat Business

Marc Graboff

F INDING MYSELF in a position of power after over twenty years in the entertainment business is both an unnerving and exhilarating feeling. One abiding principle that I follow to keep my feet planted firmly on the ground is that power is always fleeting; no one can stay in the power position indefinitely. Those who define themselves by their job titles inevitably lose their sense of self when the time comes—and it always comes—that they are no longer in a power position. One literary agent I know, who has been in the television business much longer than I and who has seen powerful people come and go in the revolving door that is the entertainment business, always tells his junior colleagues to "pitch to the chair, and not to the person sitting in the chair—they'll be gone soon enough."

Of course, that's not to say that, while one is in the chair, he or she is not made to feel as if they were the only person who had ever occupied the chair, the only person who would ever occupy the chair, and the best person ever qualified to sit in the chair. And this is where the slippery slope starts: people in positions of power can easily start believing their own press; in other words, they start believing that all the people who hang onto their every utterance and who shower them with attention, gifts, great floor seats to Laker games, and so on, are truly their friends and admirers. It becomes so easy to buy into all the publicity, accolades, and fake friendships that suddenly sprout when one's title has the word *president* in it or when you can green-light a project to production. It becomes easy to forget one's humble origins on the lower end of the entertainment business food chain and to assume that the new position of power will be indefinite.

As a result, many people in positions of power lose sight of their humble origins and, following the maxim that power corrupts, start to use that position in ways that are sometimes abusive, unethical, or downright immoral. The power is so intoxicating that many people let it become an all-consuming thing that controls every aspect of their lives; they spend all day working, and then on nights and weekends go to industry events and socialize with the very people they spend their weekdays with. All sense of balance, of perspective, and of a world outside of showbiz is lost. These are the same people who frequently become lost souls when they lose their position of power—they have so defined themselves by their prime tables at trendy restaurants and invitations to exclusive parties that when they no longer can command these things they go into deep depression.

One of the ways I try to keep myself grounded in reality is to make sure I balance my family life with my work life. It's not hard to come back down to earth after hobnobbing with famous and powerful people during the day when you have to take out the trash at night. The Hollywood life doesn't hold much appeal for me in any case—I much rather be at home at night helping my kids with their homework than socializing at the newest Hollywood hot spot.

Everyone knows the cliché: Be nice to the people you meet on the way up, because you will eventually meet them again on the way down. What constantly amazes me is that, even though this cliché has proven true time and again (I guess that's why it's called a cliché), so many people in the entertainment business either forget it or don't buy into it in the first place. No doubt, there is a culture in the entertainment business that frequently rewards bad behavior—how many times have we seen that the more ruthless, egomaniacal, and abusive a person is, the more powerful, famous, and financially successful that person becomes? These are the people who would rather live by another cliché: Nice guys (and gals) finish last. In fact, the bad-boy or bad-girl character has become a generally accepted entertainment industry archetype—a role model, if you will—that has been most recently portrayed by Jeremy Piven as the Ari Gold character in the popular HBO series *Entourage.* Many people think that Gold is a caricature of a Hollywood agent—I'm sorry to say that, in some ways, his performance is subdued. (It's also worthy of note that Gold is one of the few characters on TV who is openly Jewish; the perpetuation—albeit in an updated way—of the stereotypical immoral Jewish Hollywood agent is a matter for a whole other discussion.)

For a very long time in my career, I seriously questioned whether I would ever be able to achieve my ambition of rising to the top of an entertainment company, given that I am constitutionally unable to be that archetypal personality of the aggressive, ambitious, "take no prisoners" executive, of which there is no short supply in the business. Mainly as a result of my Jewish upbringing and how I'm wired as a person, I have a deep sense of empathy; I have always treated others as I would like to be treated myself. After moving to Los Angeles from Brooklyn, New York, as a young child, I was raised in a neighborhood with not many Jewish residents. Many of my grade-school classmates and neighborhood friends were not Jewish; and because of my religious and cultural differences compared to my classmates and friends (such as my not being available for after-school activities on Hebrew-school days or my being one of the very few students absent from school on the High Holy Days), I felt like somewhat of an outsider. I felt the most comfortable around other Jewish kids to whom I was exposed when I joined various Jewish youth organizations (such as United Synagogue Youth [USY], B'nai B'rith Youth Organization [BBYO], and Aleph Zadik Aleph [AZA]). The youth leaders with whom I interacted taught me much about what it is like to be a young Jewish American in a predominately non-Jewish society, including how to deal with feelings of inferiority and disconnectedness to the larger community and how to feel proud of my Jewishness. As a result, and coupled with my already inherent empathetic nature, I became deeply sensitive to the feelings of others—both as a way for me to deal with my own interactions with others and as a way to make other newcomers or outsiders comfortable in groups of which I was a part.

In my early years as an executive, I saw my empathetic nature as a potential liability, rather than an asset. I had no shortage of ambition; I just wanted to achieve my goals in an ethical way, on my own merits. When I was just out of college in the late 1970s, I worked as a trainee at one of the major talent agencies. The culture of the talent agency business was then, as it remains now, a culture of survival of the fittest. Governed very much like a boot camp, the trainees are subjected to endless hours and frequent abuses from some senior agents—usually for years—until, at last, the surviving trainees are granted jobs as agents, so that they can continue the vicious circle by mistreating the next batch of trainees. During the long hours, the trainees are expected to learn, almost by osmosis, the basics of the entertainment business and the skills of being an agent. I threw myself into the job of agent trainee, hoping that my brains, social skills, and work ethic would get me to the finish line of being anointed an agent.

One day, one of the founding partners of the agency called me into his office and basically told me that he didn't think I had what it took to be an agent. I'll never forget his words to me that day: "You're no Sammy Glick," the protagonist of the famous show-business novel by Budd Schulberg titled *What Makes Sammy Run?* Glick was a conniving, credit-grabbing, Machiavellian, backstabbing, pathologically aggressive character who scratched, clawed, and lied his way to the top of the ladder in show business. In short, Glick was the epitome of what a successful agent should ascribe to, according to the agent who held me up to the character's high standard and found me wanting.

I was stunned by this statement and did not know how to respond. I left the agent's office despondent and, very soon thereafter, I quit the agency business and went to law school, preferring to focus on the business side of the entertainment business, where I hoped intellect could be a more important factor for success.

While I may have been naive to think that the business side of showbiz was a pure meritocracy and that those with at least some Sammy Glick traits wouldn't pervade that part of the business, I resolved that I would always be true to my nature; the worst thing I could do was to become someone I was not. In effect, I decided that I was going to try to be a nice guy who finished first—or, at the very least, to be able to look at myself in the mirror and say that I did not compromise my values in pursuing my ambition. I realized that I may not wind up at the top of the corporate ladder, but at least I would be able to sleep at night. During my years first as a lawyer and then as a television business executive, I worked hard, used my brains to maintain my competitive advantage, and was loyal to my colleagues, earning their loyalty in return. I gradually established a reputation as an honest, straightforward dealmaker and businessperson and someone who would always deal equitably. People knew I was a man of my word; therefore, when I gave my word, it meant something. The only times I ever became one of those Hollywood "screamer" types was when someone screamed at me first or confused my easygoing nature with weakness and tried to take advantage in an unethical way. I was an example of someone with a soft heart, but a hard head.

I am very pleased that my hard work has paid off. I am in a job that I like, working with people whom I both like and respect. While I do have what could be considered a power position within my company and industry, I try never to let it corrupt my perspective or priorities or impact how I conduct myself and treat others. Too often I have witnessed otherwise gentle people become abusive because they themselves have been or are being abused by their boss. I believe the senior management of a company sets the whole tone for the culture of that company. I have worked in an organization that was led by a mercurial and abusive manager and saw firsthand how that abusive culture took root in the conduct of everyone who worked underneath that person—it was as if I worked at a company full of abused children. I left that company (and abusive culture) in part because I did not want to be a part of such a negative organization.

In my current job, I know that I, along with the other senior managers of my company, can create by our own example a culture of respect, collaboration, and equanimity that will spread to everyone within our organization. Creating and maintaining this culture is not a difficult thing: I have zero tolerance for office politics; I foster a meritocracy by which passion, intelligence, imagination, and inclusiveness are rewarded, and I strongly encourage loyalty and team spirit among all my co-workers. The individual who grandstands his or her individual achievements and distances himself or herself from the "failures" of others has no place in my organization—all of our successes and failures are shared. I also encourage people on my team to take chances—I would much rather a person try a new idea and fail than never try at all.

I look at every young staffer at my company as my future boss (not just because they could very well become my boss one day when I'll still need a job); I treat everyone with whom I deal both inside and outside my company with respect and dignity, from the most lowly assistant (especially the agency assistants, because I sympathize with their plight) to the most senior executive. I do this because it is who I am and also because I want to set an example of behavior. I want to help end the vicious circle of abused junior executives becoming abusive senior executives. I want to show the entertainment business that Sammy Glick is *not* the role model—he is the epitome of what is to be avoided at all costs. I want to prove that nice guys and nice gals *can* finish first.

When I was a member of the Entertainment Division Steering Committee of the United Jewish Federation (UJF), there was a famous (likely apocryphal) story that went around about one of the early studio founding fathers, Harry Cohn of Columbia Pictures. Cohn used to call each of his employees (even the non-Jewish employees) into his office once each year and inform them of what they each would personally be contributing to the UJF that year (whether they liked it or not). While I'm sure Cohn raised a great deal of money with that method, it is not a way that I would consider an appropriate use of my position of power (nor is it a way that, in this day and age, would allow me to keep my job). I will always encourage my colleagues to be charitable and will try to set an example of charitable behavior by not only giving money each year but also by giving my time and energy to charitable causes.

I will, however, allow my position of power to be used in one somewhat manipulative way: on occasion, I will agree to be honored by a charitable organization that I support (the most recent being the Jewish Family Service of Los Angeles). When a senior-level entertainment executive is honored by a charity, usually the TV networks, talent agencies, studios, and production companies support the event (and cause) by purchasing tables and tribute-book advertisements. How this tradition evolved is fairly obvious: the entertainment industry (like many businesses) is a relationship business. All the various constituencies in the business help maintain their relationships with each other in many ways—parties, dinners, social events, seemingly endless self-congratulatory awards shows, and, most important, mutual support of charitable causes. Rather than buying me dinner or taking me to a sporting event, I encourage those who feel the need to maintain or forge a relationship with me (or more accurately, my chair) to accomplish that same goal by supporting the charitable causes with which I am associated. Am I taking advantage of my position of power? Possibly. However, I would like to think that I am taking advantage in a moral way by channeling behavior into a more worthy form of influence peddling—charitable giving.

When I think back to that day when I was told that I was no Sammy Glick, I realize that I finally have a response to that statement: "Thank you; that's the nicest thing anyone has ever said to me."

My Experience in Raising and Dealing with Ethical Issues at Jewish Family Service (JFS)

Sandra King

Fairness

SALLY EDELIS, my associate director at Jewish Family Service of Los Angeles, and I used to do training and conferences on ethical dilemmas in agency management and case management; and a lot of the materials included in this volume remind me of that. We ran sessions for staff, for continuing education credits for social workers, and for various conferences. I also helped train students at the University of Southern California School of Social Work.

We would use case studies to talk about the dilemmas that come up when you have power over people, focusing not only on what you would do but also on the implications of reacting in one way as against another. These were the kinds of cases for which there is no one right answer, for which each thing you might do has advantages and disadvantages.

The interesting thing is that in thinking about the cases for this volume and in thinking about the broader topic of power in running an agency, I had a different take on the cases from that implied by the questions—and I tested my thoughts with Sally, and she confirmed my feelings. This volume seems to ask, "What responsibility do you have when you have power over others?" We both thought that the issues we faced were not so much corruption but the difficulty of carrying out our responsibility to be fair. Fairness is a difficult place to land when you have a variety of constituencies to whom you have to be fair. So it does not seem as clear—as a student might think when first coming into a work environment—that the power of the chief executive officer is that of being able to hire someone or fire someone; it is much more a matter of how that person finds a balance among all the conflicting needs of the people and programs involved. It is a more subtle kind of dilemma, which is powerful because it drives you in all directions.

If you have the power to affect people's lives, have the best intentions in the world, and really want to do it right (in other words, you are not corrupt), you still have many forces pulling you in different directions. Maybe two people are applying for a job: you have been friends with person *A* for forty years but person *B* has greater financial need for the job and maybe even greater competence. Sally and I both felt that, as we looked at what we had done in running Jewish Family Service (JFS), if we had any regrets about our choices and actions in very difficult situations, it was mostly around overcoming any urge to do our job in a way that was not totally fair.

Manager–Subordinate Relations

Another aspect of our moral dilemmas derived from subordinates' reticence to fight for their needs when serving their clients. We definitely did not want our subordinates to feel intimidated by us or worried that they would lose their jobs if they demanded too much. Maybe it is because we are Jewish or because we are social workers, but all too often we found ourselves having to urge our subordinates (many of whom were not Jewish) to demand what they needed for their clients or their programs or themselves. We wanted our workers to let us know what they needed and to fight for their position. Somehow, as both Sally and I were moving up the ranks in the organization, neither of us felt that there was any intimidation in JFS to prevent us from standing up to a supervisor. In fact, sometimes I wondered how Arnold Saltzman, the previous director of JFS of Los Angeles, tolerated me! Worrying about my job just never occurred to me. It just was not the nature of the game at JFS. I came into the agency when I thought that there was so much that I could do, so much that needed changing, that I felt that one just told management what was right and then changed it. Sally did and felt the same thing. Maybe it was just the nature of the two of us, but I think it was the culture of the agency as well, a culture that permitted and even encouraged frank, constructive interactions.

When I was director, as I would go around the offices to talk with the people working for the agency, I had a lot of trouble with employees who would tell me, "They won't let us." I would ask them, "Who's 'they'?" There was always this "they"—not even "you" (the director), but *they*—the city or the state or the board. When I would ask that question, some people had in mind just a nonspecific "they" out there somewhere. I don't see such people as being afraid of authority but rather of not wanting to take responsibility, because if you own something, you have to work for it. When social workers, secretaries, or anyone else working for JFS would say, "They won't let me," they were revealing their own dependency on the status quo. I much preferred people who took the initiative and stood up for what they needed or argued for ways to change something.

To create a productive environment, we diminished bureaucracy in the agency as much as possible. That meant that many, many people reported to me directly—many more than any management guru would tell you is wise—but I was willing to tolerate that level of openness and the time it took so that people would accurately feel that they were responsible for what they were doing and therefore responsible also to fight for it. That meant that my management team consisted of all the program directors (and not just one top manager in charge of programs) as well as the directors of the regions and the finance and development directors. I wanted all the decisions to be shared and close to the street, as it were. My subordinates had tremendous freedom to change things, which came along with their direct responsibility to make their part of JFS work well. They also could then feel good about themselves and their jobs. The agency has grown since I retired, and I know that there are now more layers of administration, and that may be necessary; but I think that the agency has to guard against too much structuring. I hope that employees at JFS do not lose that direct access to top managers and the freedom to try something new that Sally and I encouraged.

Manager–Board Relations: Issues, Policies, Identity, and Personnel

Issues

Power corrupts, and absolute power corrupts absolutely. One of the things I learned as a way to stay out of trouble and make JFS work was to share the power and to look to people to help with specific tasks. So, for example, when we began to get moral questions from our staff and from rabbis and others in the community, we established an ethics committee, and I used Rabbi Elliot Dorff, who specializes in ethics, to head it. The formation of the committee began with an Orthodox client who needed to go into a nursing facility but could not do so without filling out an Advance Directive for Health Care, and that raised the question of whether JFS should use the California form that asks about withholding or withdrawing life support. Sometimes the committee itself could solve the problem. If it was a board issue—for example, our relationship with a morally questionable funding source—it was best resolved through finding a way for the board to establish the appropriate policy.

Policies

I did not really feel more powerful when I became executive director; I just felt free—which is, I guess, what power is. I went through many years of not having control and of having to fight against what I felt were unrealistic restrictions and fears. There was a time of tremendous conflict within JFS, for example, when we first started with government grants. Because government money comes with the requirement that the programs funded with that money be open to whoever asks for it, whether Jewish or not, some board members and staff expressed a huge fear that if we applied for and accepted such money, we would not be able to stay Jewish. I remember the chief executive officer of the Jewish Federation Council, which in previous decades had funded about 90 percent of our budget, coming to a board meeting and saying "Beware of the government."

On the other hand, we were then getting millions of dollars from various levels of government to create and run programs that were immensely helpful to our Jewish clients, including the elderly parents of some of the same people who were unhappy about accepting government money. At that point, my predecessor as director decided that we should change our logo from a depiction of a family to a stylized Jewish star. That was wonderful, except that I was spending three-quarters of my time trying to convince state authorities at the time that we were serving everyone in the Multi-Service Senior Program (MSSP) that they had given us $2 million to run. So I went to the man who was the head of the state program and asked him whether it would make any difference if our grant application had a Jewish star as our logo. He said to me, "Why would you want to do that? Why start out with something that will cause us to question whether you will really serve everyone?" As a result—and my husband warned me that I would indeed be fired for this—I used the old stationery with the old logo for many years when applying for government grants. Every time this came up, the director and I had a war. It was crazy. Talk about ethics!

We are who we are, but it is a question about how we package it. I think we have now won that war, but people forget that there were years of real struggle, and Senior Services was seen as maverick, as changing six thousand years of Jewish history. Many thought, "What are they going to do next?" We were always nonsectarian, but it was quiet. But once we applied for government grants, the very first sentence identified us as a nonsectarian agency. I used to spend equal amounts of time trying to convince the Jewish community that we were serving enough Jews while at the same time convincing the authorities running federal, state, county, and city programs that we were nonsectarian. I am sure that my successor, the current director, does the same thing.

Identity

This raises real questions about identity. Is it only a matter of packaging who you are differently to different audiences, depending on what each is looking for? Or are you really a chameleon, changing who you are to satisfy the requirements of various funders? These are serious questions, but we worked very, very hard to be able to say no to the latter question. We deeply wanted to serve Jewish clients primarily, and we wanted our services to Jewish clients to stay recognizably Jewish. But we simultaneously needed to be open to serving non-Jewish clients to be awarded the government grants that we needed to run our programs.

Similarly, although JFS opened a kosher kitchen to serve home-bound clients and elderly clients in our adult day health care programs, we could not make it *glatt kosher* if we were going to stay within our budget. As it was, we had to supplement the money the government was giving us for each meal to make it kosher. We also had to abide by county health department rules. Doing these things enabled us to get millions of dollars in government grants to provide food for those who needed it, a large percentage of whom were Jewish because we chose to function in largely Jewish neighborhoods, but it did not make the Chabad rabbi and some of our board members happy. We had to see the reality of our situation. If we didn't win the government grants, some other agency would provide the meals, and they would not be kosher so some of our clients would be left out; furthermore, we would not be able to provide the social services that accompanied the meals programs.

When I became executive director, I felt relief because the board knew that I wanted us to pursue government programs, and they would not have hired me if they objected to that. My predecessor was used to a strictly sectarian agency, which got its money from Jewish sources almost exclusively (although there was some money from United Way) and served only Jewish clients; and he was wary of what I was doing. So I do not think I felt more powerful when I was appointed; I just felt relieved that I no longer needed to fight that battle.

Personnel

A large part of being executive director of JFS was to learn not to make the decisions myself but to get the relevant people involved to make the decisions. JFS is remarkable in that not very many people who become involved in the board come with their own agendas; the agency is everyone's agenda. Some time after I had become director, a woman who had done some good work for one of our programs came onto the board. She tried to foster allies among the board for her pet program, and she tried to get staff in trouble if they did not respond to her requests for help for that program. She was inappropriate with staff. I had a good relationship with her, but I realized that I was not able to get her to stop her personal mission. I decided that the best way to get her to realize that what she was doing was wrong was to get her involved in the strategic planning process and onto other board committees because I wanted her to learn from other board members about how to behave on my board. I think she was flattered, and I think she ultimately understood what was acceptable and what was not. She never became an ideal board member, but she certainly was much better as a result of that interaction with the other members.

Another time there was a board member who said things at board meetings that were not okay. He would talk about *goyim,* and he would use language that was not appropriate. I got some board members to talk to him. He came around a little bit; he stopped saying anything offensive out loud, but he never changed who he was. By using board members, though, I was able to make more progress than if I had tried to intervene myself, especially if I alone had tried to do so.

As CEO, you do try to shape the board. A lot of new executive directors have that problem, especially younger and newer ones. I was lucky because I was very much a known entity. Not everyone on the board loved me, but I convinced the ones who did to get more actively involved. I also had the advantage of having moved up through the ranks, and so I had allies on staff as well. A new executive director who does not have those advantages has to tread carefully for a while. Ultimately, in order to be able to function effectively, a CEO needs to get his or her allies on the board. Over the years, I also tried to get a few people *off* the board. There was someone who was very mean to the staff, and there were no prospects to change his behavior. My board presidents were very helpful in such matters. In fact, I could not have done my whole job without having tremendous allies in the office of president.

On the other hand, I remember one of our cherished board members who had considerable experience in management telling me that one of the theories of management is "Let it fester." There were things I could never accomplish with certain staff people. There were some things I let fester for ten years, and my successor is doing the same thing. There are just some things you cannot change, and so you try to contain the problem and to live with it as well as possible.

Maximizing Your Strengths, Circumventing Your Limitations

Everyone is better at some things and worse at others, and it is important to recognize that in oneself. I see now that my successor is better at dealing with the relationship between JFS and the Jewish Federation Council than I was. One reason is that my successor is a man, who is talking to other men; but my successor is also good at negotiations. I was much too outspoken, so others knew exactly where I stood. My successor is more careful in what he says, and he knows how to negotiate to get things that he wants for the agency. I think the federation saw me as an irritant; the council members always wondered what I was going to do next. On the other hand, I was always very much involved with programs, much more than my successor is. So we have different strengths, and you should play to your strengths and try to make sure that the other facets of your job do not get you into trouble—no front-page stories about you in the *Los Angeles Times*!

It is not so much that absolute power corrupts, but the person in power cannot know everything. You are not everywhere, and people do not always think to tell you what you need to know. So you have to share power. You also have to put in place some ways to get evaluations of what you are doing. For example, one of my program managers regularly asked those working for her—and those leaving for other employment—what she could do better as a manager to make their work more effective and enjoyable. That kind of conversation is very important to have at regular intervals with staff. Those of us who are neurotic have those kinds of conversations with ourselves and with others every day; that is probably too much, but we should have a regular way of gaining feedback.

For example, Sally, my associate director, told me that she thought she did not allow people enough time to grow into their positions if she felt that they were not going to make it. She too easily made it clear to people that they should leave. I, on the other hand, was at the opposite end of the spectrum; in two cases there were staff people I let stay on in management positions even though they were not doing their jobs well. One was a single mother who was still at JFS even after I left; I felt sorry for her, but her staff had to put up with things they should not have had to deal with. She was doing very well in certain areas, and so I convinced myself that she was okay, even though she was making many of her staff crazy. At a certain point her staff did not even tell me about her because they knew that I was not going to do anything about it. I did change her job, but I did not let her go.

Another person was wonderful until about a year before she left, when personal issues very much got in the way of her functioning in her job. But she had been at the agency for many years, and I had known her for all those years, and so I let her continue until she retired on her own. So I was guilty in that direction; I used my power in an unfair way. If I had confronted these two staff members more directly, things might have changed or these women might have left, but I did not use the power that I had to take action. Ideally, I would have found a way to counteract my reticence to confront people and to make changes in personnel when that was necessary.

Values

Managers definitely do have their core values. When I was working for my predecessor, he used to say to me that all I wanted was justice. I used to retort that he thought that way because all he wanted was peace! Another associate director at the time wanted love, and the fourth wanted power. When I became executive director, I told him that now I too just wanted peace; forget justice! Even so, I do feel that you really have to fight for justice in your job; it is too easy to settle for peace, even though you are sorely tempted to do that and even though you sometimes let it happen precisely because it is the easier to do that than to confront people.

Case One

I spoke with Sally about the cases presented in this volume, and we both felt that Karen does not have the right to intervene. She can certainly give a pitch for her charity. She can invite people to a lunchtime talk by somebody from United Way or the art museum. Even if the charity in question is the Jewish Federation, though, she does not have the right to pressure her staff to give. Because Jewish Family Service gets some money from the federation and from United Way, I am sure that many people in the agency and in federation would disagree with us in regard to our refusal to pressure employees to contribute to those two charities; but that is how we feel. It is another matter for board members to be required to give to the charities that support the agency, which we do. That is part of the list of duties that people assume when they agree to become board members. But that is not what staff should be expected to do.

Case Two

When both Sally and I read this case, we first thought that there had to be an error, that it was really Neil who disclosed that he liked to surf the Net for pornography, and the issue is how uncomfortable Larry, the rabbi, was with that! We both had that same response. In that, you can clearly see our positive assumptions about rabbis!

I believe that Larry may seek out personal friendships among his congregants, especially if he is in a small town. Otherwise, whom is he going to have as friends? But it is not appropriate that he should expect his friends to eat only kosher food when they go out to eat in deference to him. He needs to distinguish between friendship and business. I am currently in the process of selling my house, and I met the real estate agent socially through a friend. She is really nice, and I trust her. Sometimes she will say to me, though, "Now I am being an agent." Similarly, sometimes you are a rabbi, and sometimes you are a friend, and the expectations built into those relationships are different and must be kept distinct.

As for the pornography, Neil, as a friend, can and should say to Larry, "It's your call, but I think you are playing with fire. The kind of response you are going to get if people find out about this is going to be explosive. You really should stop doing this immediately." That's as a friend. I do not think he should tell the president of the congregation; I do not think Neil has the right to do that. Further, if he is a friend of Larry's, he should not sit on the committee negotiating the extension of Larry's contract because Neil would thereby be putting himself in jeopardy of using his personal knowledge of Larry inappropriately or, conversely, for failing to inform the board of things the members might like to know. If he is a friend, he has knowledge that should not be included in an evaluation of Larry's job performance. I am not only giving priority to the duties to friends over the duties to an organization to which I belong; I am also interested in ensuring that Neil does not put himself into an ethically untenable situation with the board, one in which no matter what he does, it is wrong.

46

I did the same thing as executive director of JFS: for my own sake, I assiduously avoided having my personal friends appointed to the board. In fact, I had some personal friends who I thought would be good for the board, but I did not even suggest the possibility. I did not want my friends discussing my job performance, my salary, and so on. I wanted to make those two worlds completely separate. I did encourage my friends to give money to the agency, to come to the fund-raising dinners for JFS, and even to volunteer for one of our programs but not to participate in a governing capacity. Everyone knew I was working at JFS, and so friends would call me when they were having problems with their elderly mothers or other family matters, but I tried to keep those worlds as separate as possible.

Even with the limited tie that I was willing to make between my friends and JFS, sometimes there were problems. Let's say that I referred one of my friends' elderly parents to a board-and-care facility run by the agency, and the parent turns out to be disruptive to the extent that neither the staff nor the other residents can stand him or her. The family wants the parent to stay there, but the staff and the other residents do not. To whom would I be primarily responsible? That is the delicate issue of fairness to which I have been alluding, and one needs both experience and wisdom to see the interests of all the parties and then to balance them correctly.

Case Three

Oy! First, you have to keep in mind that Olivia is an executive secretary, and *in that role* how can she be the most effective? The issue, in my view, is what action on her part will work best *in her role*, not what is the ultimate moral mandate that people might have to warn others of danger or to disclose inappropriate action.

1. If Peter is taking money from one budget and shifting it to another, Olivia needs to say to Peter, "I noticed that you did that, and I need an explanation as to why that is okay." I do not think she should go to anyone else about this because it is not her position to do that— although you can argue that.
2. If Peter is taking money for his personal expenses, Olivia first must create a paper trail to demonstrate that he is indeed doing that. After all, he is going to fire her if he knows that she knows but has not yet documented what he is doing. She then must go to him and

say, "Peter, I have a memo that I have written, and I have not yet sent it to anyone. I know your child is sick and all the other horrible things that are going on in your life, but I cannot live with this. So I need you to know that I have written this, and now the ball is in your court." If he does not correct the situation, she has to go to him again and set a deadline, saying that after that deadline she will need to send the memo to his superiors.

We had a case once when a clinician who had worked for JFS for many years was appointed as head of one of our regional offices. She asked whether she could hire as her secretary a woman who had good secretarial skills, who had been in jail for fraud, but who had now gone through the program of Bet Teshuvah (the Jewish halfway house in Los Angeles) and wanted to put her life together again. After consultation, we agreed to hire her as a secretary. But the regional director did not like administrative work, particularly the financial tasks associated with it, and she put the newly hired woman in charge of the office money. A year later it was discovered that the woman had stolen $10,000 from the office to give to her men friends. The regional director never once checked the office's bank account. She let the other woman take money from clients, open a bank account for the region's programs, and have full, unsupervised access to that account. That we had to fire the secretary was beyond question, but my administrative director and I felt that we also had to fire the regional director because she had been totally irresponsible in her role of managing the program, especially given what she knew of the woman's background before hiring her. My associate director for administration agreed, but another director did not want to fire her because, after all, she was not the person who took the money. I shared this with the personnel committee of the board, and they not only supported me in this but insisted that we fire the regional director. I had a total war on my hands, though, with the social work staff, many of whom knew and loved the regional director. Further, she was a lovely woman; she had just made a serious mistake that had cost the agency $10,000 of communal money. She had not only failed to check the bank account but demonstrated total irresponsibility in asking the new hire to handle the program's money in the first place. That was a bad decision not only for the program but also for the secretary because it put her in the position of being tempted to steal, as she had done before. The Rabbis of the Talmud (Pesachim 22b; Mo'ed Katan 5a, 17a; Bava Metzi'a 75b) maintain that creating temptation to do something illegal is a violation of Leviticus 19:14, "You shall not place a stumbling block before the blind"—in this case, the morally blind.

Bet Teshuvah tried to convince us not to report this incident to the police. We agreed not to do that if the woman repaid the money. She did that on an agreed-upon schedule for two months and then stopped, so we reported the theft to the police. They kept her in jail for just a few months and let her go.

3. In the third variation of this case, Olivia should go to Ruth and tell her that everyone knows what has been happening between Peter and her. If she goes to Peter, he will just deny it. In fact, Ruth may deny it too. So it depends on how Ruth wants to deal with it.

4. In the circumstances of the fourth variation of this case, Olivia has to leave her job. She simply has no other choice.

5. In the circumstances of the fifth variation of this case, Olivia can and should talk to Peter. She can also leave. It is not her job, though, to evaluate Peter's competence because she does not have the authority to do that and, moreover, she likely does not see the whole picture of his contributions to the company. This is different from the second and third variations of this case, in which Peter is clearly violating a moral norm.

Union Power and the Valuable Role of the Worker
Rachelle Smith

"May 11, 1953. To David: Let us always remember that our ideal of the perfect society will be improved upon by our children. Sincerely, Uncle Joe Belsky."

THIS INSCRIPTION, in a book called *I, the Union,* was to my father, who was a devoted executive board member of the Hebrew Butchers Workers Union Local 234 of the AFL-CIO. It was written by Joseph Belsky, vice president of the Amalgamated Meat Cutters and Butchers Workmen of North America, who was also secretary of my father's beloved union.

I grew up with the union, and all of the men involved were my uncles. Uncle Joe was special even though he was not around as much as the others. He came from Odessa, Russia, in 1904. As a new American he lived on the Lower East Side in New York City, and eventually became an attorney. He started the Hebrew Butchers Workers Union Local 234, helped start the Libertarian Party in New York, and ran for state senate and for city council. From 1949 to 1962 the Meat Cutters Union, of which our local was a part, sponsored six low-cost housing cooperatives that were built in Brooklyn, the Bronx, and Utica, New York, that house over five thousand people. The union also contributed most of the funding for a nonsectarian medical center just outside Jerusalem. The medical center is named the Joseph Belsky Medical Center.

The book *I, the Union* tells the story of American men whose social and economic lives were enriched by an organization (the union) that took them out of the bondage of the sweat shop era into a life enhanced by the promise of America. My father, David Schickler, devoted 40 years to that cause. He was idealistic and always was there to help everyone and anyone who needed help with raising wages, improving working conditions, gaining respect, or finding someone to listen. My mother and I spent many evenings alone so he could do this, and I am proud that I could be a part of his work to accomplish his ideals, because he helped change history and many lives for the better.

The union was a reaffirmation of those who cherish democracy and a rejection of those who prefer one of the forms of totalitarianism. Local 234 of the Hebrew Butchers Workers Union was one of America's militant, anticommunist labor organizations. Its history represents in miniature the saga of the American Federation of Labor (AFL).

Unions in Jewish Communal Agencies

"Let the workers organize, let their crystallized voice proclaim their injustices and demand their privileges."
—*John L. Lewis, founder, CIO*

In nonprofit agencies as well as for-profit companies, unions serve important roles. Local union leaders communicate with the membership for a number of reasons—to inform, to educate, and to learn from the members what is on their minds. But there is one reason to communicate with workers that should always be paramount, namely, to encourage, to motivate, and to inspire members to act. Union leaders want their union to be strong enough to protect the rights that their members already enjoy and to be able to improve the lives and working conditions of current members, potential members, and all working families.

The world is changing very quickly, in some good ways and in some bad. Jewish communal leaders today have all too often forgotten the economic lessons of Jewish life in America in the early and middle 1900s, when unions were largely responsible for the physical safety and job security of many Jews. People who sit on nonprofit boards have also failed to manifest proper compassion for the Jewish communal workers who make their agencies' missions come true. Jewish communal workers are the secret to raising an agency's reputation, to getting funding, and to encouraging work that is well done. The reputation of an agency depends on the service given. Unions can help both agencies and their employees accomplish their goals.

I first came to Jewish Family Service (JFS) of Los Angeles nearly 12 years ago, thrilled at the prospect of working in the Jewish community again. I had worked with Hadassah of Southern California and Los Angeles, Temple Israel of Hollywood, and other Jewish organizations as a publicist. As a Jew raised with Jewish morality, I am accustomed to giving back to my community as well as to others. Throughout my career, I have seen union membership as a plus, and so I have previously been a member of the Teamsters, the American Federation of Television and Radio Artists (AFTRA), the Screen Actors Guild (SAG), and Actors Equity.

A couple of years after coming to JFS, one of my co-workers, a social worker, was being harassed at work for no apparent reason. I asked what was wrong. He had suggested to his manager that his case load was too heavy. From that moment on he was made to feel that his work was not good or even adequate. I suggested that he and I go to the union. We did, where we met with the union's president and learned that the union was there for everyone and had remedies through its contract with JFS to deal with cases like this one. I was hooked, and my union genes kicked in. I applied to become a member of the board; and a few months later, when there was an opening, I was given an appointment. Thoughts of my father and his union activities came back into my consciousness. I wanted my father to be proud, even though he is no longer with us.

Some of my efforts in the union have concerned salaries. One of the officers of the union, whom I shall call Betty, was a 41-year-old full-time social worker with a master's of social work degree. She made so little money that she could not afford medical insurance for her two children and had to go on Healthy Families, a government insurance program for low-income families. At the same time, top executives were earning six-figure salaries.

In another case, a high-ranking executive at a large agency was chosen to be its chief negotiator. This executive, however, did not understand what the word *negotiate* means. He just tried to control and did not know how to compromise. This person was religiously observant, but his moral values did not seem to go along with his religious beliefs. How could we make him understand the value of his workforce when he was always undercutting their benefits? He would not listen to reason; he thought he was always right and would argue even if he was blatantly wrong.

Another issue is the way managers treat their subordinates. Management does not seem to have a way of disciplining unethical managers whose power has gone to their heads. Many managers abuse workers by yelling at them and talking down to them. For example, a 26-year employee of Jewish Family Service worked with two other people on the statistics for his program, but something happened and the information was deleted from his computer. He went to his supervisor, and she started yelling at him instead of trying to find out how the problem could be solved. She put him down, although the mishap was not his fault to begin with. I found out later that the verbal abuse had been going on for years and that he let it go for fear of retaliation; finally, however, the worker had had enough, and he walked out and came to the union. The supervisor had been sent to anger management school in the past, but obviously it did not work. Two more people came forward with similar horror stories.

This kind of power, used in this manner, creates fear among employees. It is rampant in some of the agencies. The Jewish communal worker is fearful of retaliation by management, verbal abuse by management, increasing workloads without compensation, and favoritism. They are not allowed to make medical appointments during work hours. The people in charge, those with the power, are not listening; they have had unlimited power for too long and therefore do not properly take the needs of their workforce into consideration.

If Power Is Not Abused, Leaders and Employees Can Produce Positive Results

In the time since I have become president of the American Federation of State, County and Municipal Employees (AFSCME) Local 800, I have learned many lessons that I use daily. These include:

> *Union power can be used to help and benefit the membership.*
> *Managers need to understand that they and their employees are ultimately on the same side, that both want the best for our workers and clients and, indeed, the agency as a whole.*
> *Happy workers are productive workers.*

To accomplish these ends, management needs to work closely with employees to hear what they are saying in order to resolve issues before they become problems. Managers also need to implement change and create good working conditions. They should involve workers in the decision-making process. As good leaders, managers should set good examples in their use of power. Management sets the tone of what filters down to the workers. Better leadership occurs if everyone is involved.

My vision of the future is one in which management and the union can work side by side for the rights of every worker in a happy and healthy environment. This benefits both management and the union. Workers are seen as allies by management in pursuing the goals of the agency. The agencies are only as good as the services they supply.

Power in Government

Judaism, Politics, and the Power of Restraint

Henry A. Waxman

F OR ME, one of the most profound tenets of Jewish ethics is that since individuals have free will, we also have responsibility for our choices and actions. As Maimonides wrote, "Free will is given to every man. . . . God does not force or decree upon them to do good or evil, it is all in their own hands" (Mishneh Torah, Laws of Repentance 5:1–3).

The Jewish way is to elevate ourselves and refine our character through the observance of mitzvot. Judaism is more about acting ethically and doing the right things than about believing the right things. God's primary concern is not that we mindlessly follow ritual but instead act decently.

How we live our lives and treat others is at the heart of the matter. Ritual obligations guide us along these lines. For example, *tzedakah*, which means "righteousness" (not charity), brings justice to others and sanctity to ourselves. The discipline of kashrut raises the most mundane acts into a religious reminder that the mere physical satisfaction of our appetite can be a spiritual act. *Shabbat* provides sacred time to refresh our body and soul. It has great meaning for me primarily as a reminder that, no matter how important I am or am supposed to be, the world can get along without me quite well for one day. It puts a lot of things into perspective.

We are encouraged to emulate Moses and Hillel, who were known for their modesty and humility. Each year, the High Holy Day liturgy forces us to acknowledge our frailty and imperfection. Man is likened to a broken shard, a fading flower, a blowing wind, and a fleeting dream. We are reminded that no one, no matter how powerful, is beyond judgment.

The mitzvot serve as a check on our arrogance, self-importance, and rationalizations to do what we want. We are required to fulfill the ethical commands and choose to overcome inclinations that are immoral or unworthy.

I have looked at the issue of governmental power in a similar way. Our U.S. Constitution was designed with a mechanism of checks and balances because our founders did not trust the concentration of power and wanted to guard against the arrogance and corruption that can result.

Jewish sources historically resist an absolute power structure in a similar way. The Bible provides for a king, but he can be appointed only with the consent of the people, he cannot amass excess wealth, and he must have a copy of the Torah with him at all times so that he is conscious that his authority is governed by law (Deuteronomy 17:16–20). In addition, it is the responsibility of the prophets to admonish any abuses of power, such as when the prophet Nathan reproaches King David for making Bathsheba a widow in order to marry her (2 Samuel 11–12).

Rabbi Joseph Soloveitchik explains that rulership is suspect because "the noblest, best intentioned ruler is affected by the glory, tribute, and power of his office. This may cause him to step over the boundary of legitimate authority. The human ego is likely to be distorted and intoxicated by a status which has no external limits."[1] He connects the biblical restrictions on the king to the well-known axiom that power tends to corrupt the one who wields it.

That axiom, "Power tends to corrupt, and absolute power corrupts absolutely," is from Lord Acton, a brilliant 19th-century historian and admirer of American democracy's system of checks and balances. (In fact, as a Catholic, Acton was nearly excommunicated from the church because he dissented from believing in the infallibility of the pope.)

Unfortunately, in the early years of the 2000s, our checks and balances have broken down. We've essentially had a power structure with one-party rule in Washington. And for a decade, the Republican congressional leadership governed with the idea that their most important job was to keep their party united, even at the expense of their constitutional responsibilities.

With scandals coming to light, Republicans hurried to pursue lobbying and ethics reform. However, these were not simply problems of a rogue lobbyist or a pack of them. Nor was it a matter of a handful of disconnected, corrupt lawmakers. The source of the problems was with the operations of Congress itself.

Since the late 1990s, and especially since 2003, the precedents, procedure, and norms that guided Congress were blatantly ignored. Rules for consideration of legislation on the House floor routinely denied members the opportunity to offer amendments, stifling dissent and legitimate debate. Bills were brought up without notice, and there was no chance for

---

1. Abraham R. Besdin, *Reflections of the Rav: Lessons in Jewish Thought*, vol. 1 (Hoboken, NJ: Ktav, 1979), 128.

members to read the legislation. House–Senate conference committees that resolve legislative differences excluded Democratic members and cut deals in private, sometimes even adding provisions never considered by either chamber.

Instead of relying on committees with jurisdiction and expertise, the Republican leadership repeatedly bypassed them entirely by bringing legislation to the floor without even a hearing. Bills approved in committee were rewritten before reaching the House floor. Any compromises were only what was necessary to get all Republicans on board, which usually meant moving to the right, even if the policy did not make sense.

The handling of the Medicare prescription drug bill is one of a number of examples of this arrogant abuse. Negotiations were behind closed doors, with Democrats excluded. Key estimates about the bill's cost were withheld by a government official who was told he would be fired if he disclosed the information. And when the bill was short of votes on the House floor, the 15-minute period allotted for the vote was extended to three hours. A Republican member was offered a bribe for his support. Now, senior citizens are trying to make sense of that law and how it affects them, taxpayers are facing costs billions higher than was originally projected, and the drug and insurance companies are coming out the big winners.

Something went very wrong. If you can play fast and loose with rules of the game in lawmaking, it becomes easier to do the same thing in other areas as well, including relations with lobbyists, acceptance of favors, and the misuse of government resources and powers. There seemed to be an attitude that because they were in charge, no one could hold them accountable.

This lack of accountability bred a culture of corruption. California congressman Duke Cunningham was convicted for accepting over $2 million in bribes. Super lobbyist Jack Abramoff headed to jail, having extorted millions from Indian tribes in a web that is remarkable in its scope. And one of his closest friends, Tom DeLay, once the most powerful Republican in the House, announced his resignation at the same time as three of his former staffers faced criminal charges.

What happened to our checks and balances? What about self-restraint and ethical guidelines? How can we restore the integrity to our system?

The most effective means to restore credibility and accountability is with oversight, which if done right can find the truth and bring real change. To quote Justice Louis Brandeis, "Sunshine is the best disinfectant."

We may not have prophets in Congress to expose abuses of authority, but we do have a constitutional obligation to serve as an independent branch of government and ask tough questions to keep ourselves and the executive branch honest.

Republicans used every opportunity for oversight to embarrass President Clinton, even holding a week of hearings on whether the Clinton administration misused its Christmas card list for political purposes. Yet, when it comes to President Bush, no scandal was too big to ignore. There were no hearings to examine whether the Bush administration manipulated the intelligence to lead us into war in Iraq; none to look into the White House leak of Valerie Plame's identity as a CIA agent after her husband, Joe Wilson, spoke out about false intelligence; none to question the treatment of detainees at Abu Ghraib, Guantánamo, and other prisons; and none to reveal the waste of billions of taxpayer money by overpaying Halliburton and other private contractors in the war in Iraq and rebuilding the areas of the Gulf Coast demolished by Hurricane Katrina.

At the same time the Congress refused to do oversight, the Bush administration acted, from even before September 11, 2001, with greater secrecy than any other administration in history—exceeding even Richard Nixon's.

In 2005, *Congressional Quarterly,* a nonpartisan magazine, reported:

> Administration secrecy has become the rule rather than the exception, a phenomenon that lawmakers, journalists, public interest groups and even ordinary Americans say has interfered with their ability to participate in government and to hold it accountable for its actions.[2]

Congressional Quarterly went on to note that some of the documents the administration withheld seemed to have little to do with the war on terrorism and a lot to do with keeping embarrassing information from the public.

Not only were many documents designated as classified, some were assigned a made-up designation—such as "secret but not classified" or for "official use only"—to keep them from being disclosed. Over the past few years of the Bush administration, documents already released by the National Archives were pulled back and reclassified as secret.

---

2. David Nather, "A Rise in 'State Secrets,'" *Congressinal Quarterly Weekly,* July 18, 2005, 1958.

No doubt our national security demands that some information must be kept secret for the good of all. What we had here, however, was an obsession for secrecy without clear standards for what should or should not be made available to the Congress, the press, and the American people. In addition, there was an inconsistent pattern of the administration pursuing some leaks of classified information but not others, according to political convenience.

Obsessive secrecy, unaccountability, intolerance of dissent, arbitrary prosecutions, and elevating politics over life-and-death policy has no place in our democracy.

While some may feel my analysis is partisan, that is not my intent. My purpose is to demonstrate that abuse of power at the individual and institutional levels occurs when rules become random and arrogance trumps accountability. In politics as in Judaism, checks and balances are needed to instill ethical behavior and protect our core values. In the great tradition of our people, we should be willing to speak truth to power and demand not just talk about reform, but real action.

Judaism and Power

Elizabeth Holtzman

I LEARNED Jewish values, not directly from the standard texts, but from my family and its history. My family was not particularly religious. Growing up, I attended High Holy Day services with my maternal grandparents and went to Hebrew school to learn the language of our ancestors, the extent of my religious training then.

Nonetheless, my parents were proud Jews and taught me not only to be proud of my heritage but to understand the virulent anti-Semitism that was so prevalent in their lives—and the need to confront and resist it. My mother and her family fled the Communist takeover in Ukraine. But they didn't emphasize the stories of the government's seizing my grandfather's store or my mother's being evicted from the *gymnasium* (high school) because she came from a bourgeois family. Instead, it was the stories of my mother's overcoming the czarist quotas on Jews and winning admission to the *gymnasium* in Belaya Tserkov by studying hard and persevering, an amazing achievement that we heard again and again. Then there were the stories of the pogroms, in which Jews from the town fled to my grandfather's house, the only Jewish house on the main Christian street, to seek shelter. My mother didn't want them to stay—it was too dangerous—but my grandfather shrugged her concerns aside. Reaching for his wallet, he told those huddled there that they could remain if they wished and that he would do everything possible to save them, including paying whatever money he had, even though he made it clear that he couldn't guarantee their lives. Everyone survived.

My mother also told about the time when, on the way home from school, she was confronted by a Cossack with a rifle during a pogrom. Not sure if she was Jewish, and therefore someone he could victimize, he ordered her to pronounce a Russian word with R's in it. Jews generally pronounced the R in a German/French style, but my mother spoke perfect Russian and calmly gave him his rolled R right back. He cursed at her, but let her go.

This was the power I learned about from my family—the ability to confront, to outwit, and to overcome evil. It always seemed to me that those who had the real power were not the pogromchiks or the anti-Semites, but those who stood up to them.

My grandfather also led some 70 Jews, mostly relatives, but also business partners and friends, out of the Soviet Union in a daring escape to Romania and then to the United States in 1921. Money gave power to flee from the brute forces of anti-Semitism, but money and status were fleeting things and could vanish abruptly. My grandfather came to America, giving up a comfortable life with servants, a nice house, and carpets on the floors. Here, he started selling textiles on the sidewalk, graduated to a pushcart, and then to a small store on the Lower East Side in New York. As a Jew, you knew—or had to know—that overnight you could go from comfort to poverty. That is why education, which was portable, was the most important possession.

My next experience with the concept of power came when I went to Albany, Georgia, to work as a law student for a black civil rights attorney in the early days of the civil rights movement. There I saw the power of the "weak," in this case African Americans. They were courageously opposing the system of segregation that demeaned them. They peacefully demonstrated, picketed, and tried to register people to vote. They were willing to be arrested over and over—and sometimes beaten or mistreated—for these lawful activities.

The nonviolence of the civil rights movement turned out to be all powerful—those who were unarmed won out against those who were armed, against those with the cattle prods and the dogs, the water hoses and the jails—all of which had a tremendous effect on me. If that could happen in the South, why couldn't it happen elsewhere? Moral resistance, I discovered, could be an awesome force.

Perhaps it was no surprise that a number of the white people who came south were Jews. They understood the evil of discrimination and knew they couldn't stand on the sidelines. So it was a Jew, Zev Alony, who was one of four charged with a capital crime, trying to overthrow the state of Georgia, for participating in a peaceful voting rights march in a small town called Americus, near Albany. He and others were brutally beaten, and I was designated to go to Washington with the bloody shirts to call for federal help. No help came. But the civil rights workers didn't give up. Ultimately, the cases were thrown out, and despite horrific resistance, voting rights came to Georgia.

My earliest experience with political power was in the administration of Mayor John Lindsay of New York, where as a young (26-year-old) assistant to the mayor, I could participate in setting priorities for the parks department. To help the mayor win reelection, I wanted to put safety matting under swings and slides in all playgrounds—and they were installed; I wanted a mini-pool program, and the pools got built. This was heady stuff.

When I ran for public office, it was an outgrowth of my Jewish values. Election, I believed, would give me an opportunity to stand up more effectively against public wrongs and try to right them. My family's history and my civil rights experience made me an optimist about the possibility of changing things.

Getting elected wasn't so easy. When I ran for Democratic state committeewoman, I had to challenge the election laws, because they allowed incumbents to be placed first on the ballot, meaning that no challenger could win. I sued—the name of the case was *Holtzman v. Power*—and I won. The law was declared unconstitutional.

Power to change things by court cases was something I learned in the civil rights movement, and I was surprised but glad that I could carry that lesson from Georgia to Brooklyn. I saw the power of the courts again, in Congress and as district attorney. In Congress, I challenged President Nixon's illegal bombing of Cambodia, along with four pilots who were flying the B-52 bombers. We won in the federal district court, the first decision ever in the history of the United States to hold any presidential war making unconstitutional. We won a further order halting the bombing from Supreme Court Justice William O. Douglas, but we lost in the end when other justices, who wanted to keep the bombing going, violated the spirit of the Court's own rules by in effect overriding Douglas without the required quorum. As Douglas predicted, deaths would result; 100 Cambodians, in a village friendly to the United States, were bombed within days of the override.

I saw it happen as district attorney when we filed a friend-of-the-court brief to get the law permitting marital rape declared unconstitutional, and New York's highest court followed the legal road map we created. Most important was the role my office and I played in getting the courts to ban the practice of removing blacks from juries by means of peremptory challenges. We litigated the matter through state and federal courts, and though the Supreme Court didn't hear our case, one of the justices noted the contribution we made. I sought support from other prosecutors around the country to stop this discriminatory practice, but no one would join us.

As district attorney, I had the sole power to do some things, such as promoting women and minorities to top positions in the office. Making these changes, effectuating progress, was exhilarating. But sometimes, the use of power, even for good ends, was a very lonely task. For example, to address police misuse of force, I created a special unit, only to be picketed by 5,000 police officers. I sat in my office, sorry that it had come to this point but firm in my resolve to keep the unit operating. I thought of the police brutality I saw in the South and of the brutality of police forces against Jews in Europe, and I knew I was doing the right thing. Properly used, police power was vital; abused, it was intolerable.

Power is not simply physically changing things such as institutions, practices, or programs; it can also entail changing people's attitudes and ideas.

When I arrived in Congress in 1973, I was placed on the House Judiciary Committee, which was later to sit on the impeachment of President Richard Nixon. I marveled that a Jewish woman, the first generation of her family to be born in America, was going to be judging a president of the United States. I tried to get the committee to adopt an article of impeachment against President Nixon for carrying out the secret bombing of Cambodia, a neutral country, and deceiving Congress and the American people. I did not succeed.

Then, when President Ford pardoned Richard Nixon and appeared before a House subcommittee to explain his actions, I was the only person willing to ask President Ford the tough questions about the pardon, including whether he had a deal with Richard Nixon on the pardon. I was very reluctant to confront the president and hoped that someone who preceded me on the subcommittee would do so. But they didn't. I was the last to question, having the least seniority. So when my turn came, even though I wasn't sure what the repercussions would be, I knew that the questions had to be posed.

Although I was attacked editorially, people in New York hugged me. They wanted to see someone in office recognize that the president had done something terribly wrong and not simply acquiesce with a smile.

More than 30 years later, an incident happened that led to my standing up to a president again. One cold December morning in 2005, I picked up the *New York Times* in front of my house, and I read to my horror that President Bush had engaged in a program of what appeared to be illegal wiretapping of people in the United States. One of the grounds for the House Judiciary Committee's article of impeachment against Richard Nixon was that he engaged in illegal wiretapping. Bush was doing the same thing. I knew I had to act. Fortunately, *The Nation,* a progressive magazine, asked me to write an article, and I did so. Although impeachment had been discussed in the blogs, the concept hadn't received wide attention. No credible public figure supported it. My article helped ignite a broader national debate on the issue and led me to write a book, *The Impeachment of George W. Bush,* which I hope has enhanced the debate further. In challenging presidential misconduct and presidential contempt for the rule of law, I felt fervently that I was following in the footsteps of my ancestors.

Unfortunately, I have too often seen others fail to use the power they had to prevent injustice or wrongdoing, and I have seen power misused, even against me. Confrontation is hard and unpleasant, and too many people will take no risks for principle. So just as I saw Democrats fail to investigate the Ford pardon, I saw them more recently refuse to stand up against the war in Iraq, the torture and mistreatment of American war detainees, and the wiretapping and its undermining the rule of law in this country.

When I publicly criticized a judge for mistreating a rape victim in court by allowing her to get on her hands and knees to reenact the rape, the judges of New York twisted the rules—and ignored the First Amendment—to find that I, not the judge, violated ethical standards. It was, they claimed, improper to make my concern public. The judge was never penalized, although he was later removed from the bench in connection with an unrelated corruption scandal.

Even though I have paid a price for being outspoken and fighting injustice, I wouldn't have changed what I did at all. I learned both from my grandfather and from Police Chief Laurie Prichett in Albany, Georgia, that there are situations in which confronting authority can involve risking your life. When they don't, the choice to oppose abusive power is, for me at least, not much of an issue.

I want to add one final word about my work on Nazi war criminals. When I came to Congress, I had no idea that Nazis were living in the United States and that the government knew and was doing nothing about it. In 1974, when a whistle-blower informed me, I inquired and discovered that it was true, at which point I became the first member of Congress to point out the problem. It is a fair question to ask why nothing had been done since the end of World War II about this problem and why it was left to a brand-new member of Congress to tackle. I spent the balance of my three terms in Congress ensuring that there was a proper legal framework and a solid administrative structure to bring the Nazis to justice. I helped create a special office in the Department of Justice to track down and deport Nazis (there are constitutional limits on prosecutions in the United States for the actual crimes) and strengthened our laws. Since 1979, more than 100 cases have been brought against Nazi war criminals in the United States.

I also believed that we had to have the whole story of U.S. collaboration with Nazi war criminals. Now, Congress has enacted a law requiring that the government's secret files on Nazi (and Japanese) war criminals be declassified and made available to the public. More than eight million pages have been declassified, although not without some serious battles particularly with the CIA. (I was appointed to the panel overseeing the declassification.) These files confirm that after the war, the United States collaborated with, employed, and protected Nazi murderers from justice. Making our government act even years later in prosecuting the criminals and in declassifying the documents helps demonstrate that officials' tolerance of killers of Jews cannot go unpunished and hidden forever.

In Jewish history, the little power we had was too often focused on survival. Perhaps no other people have seen power used so viciously and persistently against them. In modern times alone, we were killed by Crusaders, expelled from almost every country in Europe, slaughtered in pogrom after pogrom, and decimated—six million of us—in the Holocaust, along with our culture, our language, and a millennium-old way of life. That history should inject us with a healthy dose of skepticism about power. It should teach us also to be especially sensitive to the security of other Jews. As important, we must remember the pain inflicted on us in our history—and vow never to inflict it on others. We need to remember what Hillel said about power: "Do not do unto others as you would not have them do unto you." And if we see that maxim violated, especially in a political context, then we cannot be silent bystanders. "Justice, justice shall you pursue" (Deuteronomy 16:20). That must be our watchword.

Power in the Professions

The Unique Role of a Physician

Aaron J. Feingold

I AM A cardiologist, practicing medicine in New Jersey. The purpose of this essay is to show how my personal relationship with Judaism has determined and shaped how I use my power as a physician.

Michael Gold's *Jews without Money* (1930) is quoted in the spring 2006 issue of *Heeb* magazine. Gold wrote of the power given to doctors in early-20th-century New York: "In the old country the Jews worshipped their rabbis. In this country the doctor was a community idol. I have seen women follow a young East Side doctor on the street, kiss his hand humbly, sob, and loudly call down God's blessing on his head as though he were a savior." Although this historical description may appear dated, it in fact portrays the regard in which physicians are held under certain circumstances and implies the power they may have over their patients.

In 1970, as a 19-year-old college junior, I got on an airplane for the first time, left New Jersey, and flew to Israel. Needing an academic break, I had petitioned the college where I was enrolled to allow a trimester independent study living on a kibbutz and creating a written and photographic journal. Off I went, ready for adventure and a new and exciting experience. I was assigned to a kibbutz in the Jordan Valley, specializing in large banana growth, and my job, because I appeared tall and strong, was to carry the large banana bunches on my back to a waiting trailer. For three months I most happily toiled in the cold, muddy, rainy season of a Galilean Israeli winter, my mind soaking up everything I saw and looking for deeper meaning everywhere. Not yet knowing the meaning of an epiphany, I certainly had an instant, immediate idea pushing into my head one day as I carried a large banana bunch: the only career in life that would meet my current existential dilemma was to be a doctor. I remember the very moment of this thought, and in my life I can say that the rest is history. Not wanting to be a rabbi, I reasoned that the only "ultimate good" was to help people stay alive through medicine. Reaching for a simplistic utopian view under the influence of the kibbutz, I intuited that being a doctor would allow me to travel and live in the United States, Israel, or wherever I wanted, this being a portable and necessary profession. This deduction allowed me to continue the mental love affair I was having with Israel and permitted dreams of a future that was not restricted to the United States in the way that other careers might be.

I did not realize it at the time, but my epiphany was part of the Jewish medical tradition and continuum. It is said that 213 of the 613 commandments in the Torah deal with health, and one of the most compelling passages is "Choose life" (Deuteronomy 30:19). We look to the past to know where we are going in the future. The power of Jewish medicine has been an historical truth since biblical times.

I find strength in this historical continuum. In the desert, Moses told the Israelites that if they looked up at his staff and the serpent upon it, they would be cured. Perhaps this was the first psychosomatic cure, and the look up was toward heaven and God's cure. This was also the first use of the serpent as a medical symbol. More important, it depicts the Torah's knowledge of the mind–body relationship and a contemporary direction for a physician's use of power.

In a famous letter written in 1199, the great Jewish physician Maimonides describes his most harrowing days practicing medicine in Cairo and Fustat. He punctuates his descriptions by describing his role as teacher, scholar, and leader of the Jewish community. The reader of this letter understands that both esteemed physician and Jewish scholar are interwoven and inseparable. His strength to practice medicine and the direction of his resultant power come from his relationship with Judaism. It is this example, provided by Maimonides, of a harried physician called in all directions at once but never acting without a reliance on Judaism, from which I draw much needed inspiration and strength as a modern-day, busy doctor.

Jewish doctors have been the translators and transmitters of medical knowledge across borders and continents and through the millennia. Using Maimonides as an example, Jewish doctors have traditionally used their power to intercede for the Jewish people with sultans, popes, kings, emperors, and politicians. Their strength and standing in a community gave them unique power and influence with the mighty. Basically translated to today, this might mean helping a Jewish day school get approval for land use expansion or a new synagogue built in a residentially zoned neighborhood. "My Jewish doctor is the best," I still hear monthly. The unique role the physician has with his or her patients extends this power to areas outside of medicine.

I am a collector of Judaica, and years ago one of my antiques dealers asked me if I wanted to bid in a London auction for a "Jewish medical book." "What's that?" I said, and won the bid. I had bought a spectacular book published in Venice in 1559 by the Murano physician Amatus Lusitanus. In his book, Amatus wrote a medical oath mostly describing his unjust persecution and reaffirming the use of his medical powers through a Jewish medical perspective. It struck me that his ethical concerns and focuses were as relevant today as they were in 1559 or in the time of the Bible and that they would be relevant 1,000 years into the future. For example, Amatus swears by God and the Ten Commandments that he has never practiced deception. He has never revealed a secret. He has never given a fatal draft. He has never brought about an abortion. He has not practiced base conduct in the house of a patient. These are concerns and limits on the use of power that we, as Jewish doctors, can look back at and feel a historical and ethical bond.

Being absolutely blown away by this Jewish medical link to the past, I next purchased a book found in a dusty bookstore in an alley in Paris. The book, *Otzar ha-Hayim* (*The Treasure of Life*), was written by rabbi and physician Jacob ben Issac Zahalon and published in 1683. Zahalon made his living as a physician but was the chief rabbi of Rome. (It is interesting that the chief rabbi of Rome today is a radiologist.) Zahalon published a scientific text but established the physician as an instrument of God's work. He placed disease and its cure exclusively within God's decree and plan: "Thou art the physician, not I." It struck me that with this one sentence Zahalon explained why in modern times some patients are helped and cured and others do poorly despite the same treatment. Looking back at such physicians, we see a portrait of humility and a direction for the use of our power today.

Knowledge of the history of Jews in medicine has given me terrific strength to deal with modern medical problems. It has given me conviction to recommend the study of medicine to young people, despite an increasingly bad regulatory environment and the lack of the instant financial windfall that might be gained on Wall Street. "We are on the side of the angels," I tell them. The percentage of doctors represented by the perhaps 125,000 Jewish physicians in the United States greatly outnumbers the percentage of Jews in the overall population. These doctors need to know that much of why they ended up becoming a physician is because they are Jewish. Whether this is due to a Darwinian developmental gene or socialization, it is the truth.

When I reflect, my religious attitude shapes the everyday use of my power as a physician. Physicians have a constant fear of abuse of this power. Patients usually trust, follow, and obsessively obey their physicians. What drives the formation of our medical ethics and our implicit need to follow them? The Decalogue, or Ten Commandments, which most Jewish physicians learn as children, seems the foundation of medical ethics, containing, as it does, the instructions for most ethical questions. Physicians should not lie, murder, or commit theft. If I recommend a treatment to a patient, I will tell the truth and not be motivated by other factors, such as financial reward. Thus if I recommend a coronary angioplasty instead of cardiac surgery, this must not be because I gain financially from the angioplasty. A surgeon may be the best technical operator, but if he or she lies, and says, for example, that there is a cancer when the tumor is known to be benign, then the surgeon abuses his or her power. This is why hospital credentials committees evaluate truthfulness as being as important as surgical ability. We have the power to save a life—or to screw it up. This is the fear faced every day by the physician. I find solace in the talmudic recognition of this: "The best of physicians are destined for Gehenna." My interpretation of this talmudic phrase is that even the best doctors can make disastrous mistakes. Recommendation for hospice, or end-of-life care, always frightens me, lest I give up on a life too soon. We have the power to suggest prayer, and I often do.

Religious attitudes shape the everyday use of power in the practice of medicine. Sometimes, I think to myself that just practicing medicine to an ethical standard replaces the need for prayer.

For myself, connecting my Jewish identity with my practice of medicine has become a passion. I have participated in medical missions to such places as Ukraine, Hungary, and Cuba, offering medical assistance to Jewish communities in need. I joined the American Physician Fellowship for Medicine in Israel in 1976, while I was still an intern, volunteering to go to Israel as a doctor in time of emergency. In 1995, I was chairman of an event hosted by the American Friends of Beth Hatfutsoth at the Plaza Hotel in New York to honor Dr. Jonas Salk for his contributions to humanity. From the podium, Salk said: "Being Jewish has always been the most important unconscious force in my life." I must agree with Salk, who is the discoverer of the polio vaccine that saved millions of lives. Being Jewish has been the moving force in my life; and every day, as I practice medicine, it provides me with perspective, strength, and direction for the use of my power.

Learning to Teach: Reflections on the Transition from Student to Teacher

Daniel Held

I N THE September, 2005, after my college graduation, my life changed. I began my first full-time job. From kindergarten through college, I had always been in a position of subordination to my teachers. It was, after all, they who would take attendance, mark my tests, and—God forbid—call my parents. Everything I did (or didn't do) was marked in the teacher's notebook and stored for future use. Now, as a young teacher, the tables had turned. There I was, my first full-time job, my first step outside the power dynamic of being a student, my first classroom, and my first set of students.

Growing up, I remember examples of the power my teachers exerted over me. On the Jewish holiday of Tu b'Shevat, my Hebrew teacher explained that around the world Jewish students mark the holiday by planting trees in Israel. She would then hand out an envelope and expect us to return it the next day, forms completed and money in hand. Who was I to say no? After all, the teacher, the moral authority and the assigner of A's, B's, and F's, was asking me to make a donation.

Similar episodes took place during college. I remember a professor, at the end of a lecture, announcing a protest rally taking place the next day and saying, "I hope to see you there." Surely the professor, a learned scholar whom I respected, is rallying for an important cause that I should support. Moreover, if the professor hopes to see me at the rally, does the cause really matter? Even if I disagree with the issue, does my opinion take precedence over the fact that the professor might note my absence?

My student life was filled with similar scenarios as my teachers, principals, and professors held positions of power over me. As a young student I wasn't able to recognize the nuances of the situation or identify the pressures that were placed on me. Rather, it was clear that if my teacher, whom I admired, feared, and respected, said I should be doing something, then it should be done. It was only during high school and college, as I began to think independently and critically, that I recognized the power that my teachers exerted.

Then I graduated from college. Suddenly the tables were turned, and the power relationship, to which I had become so accustomed, was set upside down. No longer was I the student, but now the teacher. I had been in positions of power before—as a camp counselor, babysitter, student teacher—this, however, was to be the first time that I had my own class. I was going to teach students, take attendance, grade papers, assign marks, and—if need be—call parents. My new responsibilities came with a new position of power.

I spent the summer agonizing over my first day. How would I present myself? What rules would I set? It became clear to me that teachers hold two forms of power over their students. These two types of authority can be demonstrated through the cases of Karen, the Jewish vice president of the investment firm, and Larry, the newly ordained rabbi.

Karen has the power to hire and fire, give bonuses and raises, assign work and demand results. She therefore holds what I term "structural authority." Any interaction that Karen has with her employees is governed by this inequality in their relationship and by the structural power that Karen holds over her employees. In the case of Karen asking her employees to make a charitable contribution, one has to realize that her request will be viewed as a request from "the boss." How can you say no when your boss, the person who has the power to fire you, makes the request?

At the same time, however, complex interpersonal relationships are governed by multiple interactions. Karen is not only the supervisor but is also another human being. When making requests of her employees that are not related to work, Karen must transparently disassociate herself from her position of structural authority. Perhaps that means doing it during lunch or outside of work hours. Perhaps it means specifically articulating that a charitable contribution is not a work-related expectation.

I was faced with a similar situation a few months ago. My boss was participating in a walk-a-thon to raise money for cancer research. Instead of individually approaching employees for sponsorship, she posted the information on the staff bulletin board. She diminished the coercive nature of the request by posting the information rather than by approaching each employee and having him or her make a decision on the spot.

As a teacher, I hold structural authority over my students. Although, I cannot fire them (though sometimes I may want to), I do write report cards and assign grades. I too have to be careful with my use of structural authority. When asking my students to do something noncurricular—planting trees for Tu b'Shevat, carrying a heavy pile of books to the library, or helping me with computer problems—I must be clear that these requests are not linked to their academic performance—just as

Karen must be clear that charitable contributions are not related to her employees' job performance.

The case of Larry, the newly ordained rabbi, presents another dilemma of power. While he does not hold structural authority over his congregants, they do invest in him another type of power—"moral authority." Because of Larry's learning and actions, his congregants choose to place him in a position of respect and therefore invest within him moral authority. As opposed to structural authority, which is assigned based on external criteria, such as the power to hire or assign a grade, moral authority is determined by the individual. Through the course of experience each of us decides, for himself or herself, whom we put in positions of moral authority.

I personally hold certain rabbis, teachers, community leaders, and relatives in positions of moral authority. Over the course of time, their actions and advice have elevated their status in my eyes. I often turn to them to ask questions of ethics and morality and, in some respects, attempt to emulate their behavior. While I am not bound by their advice, the authority that I have chosen to invest in them adds to their credibility.

The authority I place in moral role models changes as I learn more about the individuals and as our relationships develop. Teachers whom I adored in high school may hold less relevance in my adult life. As time passes since my last interactions with these moral authorities, their power may diminish. In some cases, male politicians for whom I voted were later found to abuse their power over women, and business leaders whom I idolized were charged with fraud. New insights into the lives of these moral authorities have affected the power that they hold over me.

Similar changes take place in the opposite direction. A wealthy member of my community, whom I always thought of as stingy, was recently revealed as the anonymous benefactor of several important projects and today serves as an example for philanthropy. When reminiscing about our high school days, a friend told me wonderful stories about the empathy and caring of a particular teacher with whom I never connected. I e-mailed the teacher, and our relationship has since blossomed. Because of the perspective my friend shared, I now view that teacher as one of my mentors. Seeing who others hold as moral authorities influences who I place in that position.

In my mind, Larry's disclosure of his enjoyment of surfing the Internet for pornography drastically changes his position as a moral authority.

Neil was alarmed by Larry's hobby, and it diminished Larry's moral power over Neil. Acting as a moral authority is one of the most important roles of a rabbi. To this end, I believe that Neil can, and should, raise his concerns with the president of the congregation and the contract committee because Larry's fixation on pornography directly impacts one of his functions in the community. We must hold rabbis, politicians, and community leaders accountable to the respect that their office and community command of them.

As a teacher, some of my students may place me in a position of moral authority. I consider myself to be a *dugma ishit,* a "personal example," and recognize that my actions, like those of Larry, are observed and cataloged by my students. I believe that both in and out of the classroom, I not only teach the curriculum but also lessons in humanity.

The clearest example of these lessons is modeling positive interactions with others. In this I am guided by Leviticus 19:18, "Love your fellow as yourself." One could easily suggest that in an unequal power relationship, the two parties cannot be considered "fellows." In my class, however, I adopt the philosophy that if I expect respect from my students, I must offer them the same treatment.

Rabbi Akiva later paraphrased the biblical commandment to "what is hateful to you do not do unto others" (Babylonian Talmud, Shabbat 31a). The subtle difference is important in shaping my relationship with my students. It has not been long since I was a student myself. When teaching, I try to think what the class would be like if I were on the other side of the desk, if I were the student subordinate to the teacher. I believe that a similar attitude should be adopted in other relationships. If Karen could put herself in the shoes of her employees and recognize the pressures that she puts on them by asking for donations, she would be better equipped to find an alternative way to ask for the money.

The power relationships I create with my students are modeled on two other sets of relationships described in the Bible: with one's parents and with God. In both cases, classical texts create models for a spectrum of authority between unequal partners.

Both when living at home and when out of the house, my parents have played a major role in my life. Their power stems not only from being the keeper of the car keys and the enforcer of the curfew but also by being the people to whom I turn when things go wrong. They have guided me by finding a delicate balance between acting as structural authorities, who grounded me when I did wrong, and as moral authorities, whom I respect and try to emulate in countless ways.

Over time, the power relationship with my parents has changed. The greatest change occurred when I moved out of their house and my parents no longer used punishment as an expression of their structural authority. At the same time, however, my parents' role as moral authorities shifted as I grew to see them in a new light. Like every child, I used to view my parents as "super-people" who were stronger and smarter than any other parents in the world. As I grew older, I began to realize that my parents were human, and their individuality manifested itself through their own unique strengths and weaknesses. Growing up living with my parents, I knew more about them than anyone else. I observed their every move, their decisions, conversations, and relationships. Each of these informed their position as a moral authority in my life. Today their authority, while more distant than it used to be, holds considerable weight, and I often turn to myself wondering what my parents would do in a given situation.

The Torah sets out a dichotomy of child–parent relationships. In the Ten Commandments, the Bible prescribes that one must "honor your father and your mother" (Exodus 20:12; Deuteronomy 5:16). The term *honor* connotes a relationship of respect through warm admiration. Conversely, shortly before the charge to "love your fellow as yourself," the Torah dictates, "You shall each revere his mother and his father" (Leviticus 19:3). The wording in this case reflects a respect through fear and awe of one's parents. These two statements represent different positions along the spectrum of a parent's power.

A similar dichotomy is demonstrated through the relationship between God and the Jewish people. God, whom I believe holds the ultimate power both as a structural authority who can reward and punish and as a moral authority who is just and principled, is described as holding two conflicting attributes: *middat ha-din,* the attribute of "strict justice," and *middat ha-rachamim,* the attribute of "mercy." Classical commentaries on the Torah identify God as acting with each of the attributes at particular episodes in the Bible. When Adam was exiled from the Garden of Eden, God was acting on his attribute of strict justice. After the sin of the Golden Calf, however, when God considered wiping the Israelites off the map but chose not to do so, he exercised his attribute of mercy. Both *middat ha-din* and *middat ha-rachamim* are expressions of

God's power—one through strict authority and the other through merciful understanding.

In my classroom, I emulate these two relationships. At times I model *middat ha-din* by strictly enforcing my power. I insist that the students face forward, take notes in a particular way, hand in assignments on time, and so forth. In these instances, I expect from my students strict obedience and reverence modeled on the parent–child relationship of Leviticus. These are all expressions of my power gained through emphasizing the unequal status of the student and the teacher. At the same time, however, I recognize that the student–teacher relationship includes *middat ha-rachamim*—attributes that are more gentle. When a student approaches me for an extension on an assignment, when he needs to take a few minutes for himself, or when a student is struggling in class, I purposely moderate my position of authority to offer greater empathy and patience. In these cases, I try to develop a level of warm respect modeled after the Ten Commandments paradigm for parent–child relationships. I minimize the inequality in our power relationship to be more empathetic to the needs of the student.

When preparing for my first classroom and thinking about my relationship with my students, I spent a tremendous amount of time considering the broad range of possibilities that could exist. I spoke with friends and mentors, with family and students. I explored biblical and rabbinic literature and reread education textbooks from college. After my first year of teaching, however, I realized that there is no one paradigm for power relationships that can be applied across the board. Every moment of every day, the power dynamic between people changes. Karen's authority during the workday is different from that during a lunch break; Larry's relationship with Neil shifts from the synagogue to the tennis court; and our relationships with God and our parents change. Each is based on a thousand factors of time and circumstance.

I realize that one day I may express my power in class firmly and another day I may be more subtle. Similarly, I know that sometimes I will be too lenient and sometimes too harsh. I know that I will make mistakes. In preparing to make the shift from student to teacher, however, the most important thing I learned is that there is no one ideal archetype for power relationships. As long as I continue asking questions about my use of power, I will continue to grow as an educator and as an individual.

When Power Is Resisted

Gail Labovitz

I N THE early days of the Internet, when I was a recently ordained rabbi working on a doctorate at the Jewish Theological Seminary, I participated in an e-mail discussion group for Conservative Jews. There is one discussion I remember in particular. A man wrote about trying to balance his identities as a gay man and as an observant Jew in a religious system that has historically declared homosexual behavior to be a violation of Jewish law. Having decided that Jewish law should take primacy, he had joined an Orthodox synagogue. Moreover, he framed his choice in terms of power and powerlessness: he had, he felt, deliberately put himself in a place of powerlessness, subordinating his romantic and sexual desires to his commitment to Jewish law and practice.

I grew up as a Conservative Jew. During college I became more religiously observant and spent some time exploring Orthodox lifestyles and participating in Orthodox communities. I was never able, however, to harmonize my upbringing in a lay-led minyan (a worship community), in which women participated equally with men, with the gender segregation I found in Orthodox prayer services (and its religious leadership roles). When I was required to sit behind a *mechitzah,* a "partition" separating men and women, while men led the services and took all the ritual roles, I felt powerless. Rather than experiencing this form of Jewish life as worthy submission to God and tradition, I felt I was being cut off from serving God as fully as my education and abilities would allow. My male correspondent had voluntarily chosen to join a community that I experienced as disenfranchising to me and all its female members. *He* felt powerless in an Orthodox synagogue? He was on the side of the *mechitzah* where all the action was!

I thought carefully about what he had written and what I wanted to write back. In my reply, I considered what it would be like for the two of us to meet in person at his Orthodox synagogue. On the men's side of the *mechitzah,* he would be able to lead services and read from the Torah—but at the price of having to hide an essential element of his identity. It is a mitzvah, a "religious obligation," for Jews, especially men, to marry and have children. How would the community react to a man who was unwilling to fulfill this mitzvah and how could he explain himself to them? Meanwhile, over on the women's side, I could participate only passively in religious services, but I would be recognized and respected as a wife and mother of two young children, a model member of the community. Each of us, then, would have a form of power in that place that the other lacked, and each of us would have relinquished some form of power to be there.

At that point, our conversation veered off into other issues. But in the decade-plus since then, I have continued to think about our initial exchange and what it might have to teach about power and its workings. What I would add now to my analysis of our imaginary meeting in the Orthodox synagogue is a reminder that no matter how we might have related to each other, neither of us would have had full access there to the power that the community granted to heterosexual men. On the other hand, if we each continued to participate regularly in that community without challenging the ways in which it distributed power, one could argue that we would both be complicit in perpetuating that power structure. In fact, we have seen a great deal of social change even in Orthodoxy over the last two decades, as women, and supportive men, advocate for the Orthodox world to change its practices and/or develop new ones, through activities such as forming women's prayer groups and creating places for women to engage in advanced religious studies.

As already suggested, I myself could not remain in the Orthodox world. I chose instead to return to my Conservative roots and even to seek a position of leadership and influence in the movement by studying to be a rabbi. And yet, here's another lesson about power that I learned from my own movement, also shortly after my ordination. In the fall of 1993, I helped organize a conference at the Jewish Theological Seminary (JTS) to mark the tenth anniversary of the decision to admit and ordain women at its rabbinical school. One of the sessions during the two-day event was dedicated to a discussion of "pluralism." This is an important concept to us Conservative Jews; we regularly use the term as shorthand for our commitment to allow and respect multiple interpretations of Jewish law (for example, some of us drive to synagogue on Shabbat, others of us consider this a violation of Sabbath prohibitions, but both are considered valid positions within the movement). At this session of the conference at JTS, however, several speakers took this term and this topic as an occasion to stress the importance of maintaining a place in the movement for those who do not accept women's full ritual participation or women's ordination. It took some time for me to put into words why this felt so hurtful and wrong—and why I was suddenly feeling so powerless, despite my title and my role in this conference. I stood up and asked: "If pluralism is a value of inclusiveness, what sort of inclusiveness is built on defending others' right to exclude, to exclude *me* and all my female colleagues? What does it mean to have put in all the work and learning needed to earn the title 'rabbi,' only to have my own colleagues tell me that I cannot count in a minyan with them, or be called to the Torah, or to lead services in their synagogues, or have them recognize the conversions in which I participate?"

Today, more than a decade later, I am not only a rabbi but also a scholar of rabbinics. Moreover, in my current position at the Zeigler School of Rabbinic Studies at the American Jewish University, I participate intimately in the training of rabbis-to-be. I am gradually realizing my place as a leader in my community, with power to influence its direction and future. And yet, the same questions about pluralism, nonegalitarianism, and whether women can fully fill the role of rabbi continue to surface again and again among Conservative Jews. I was saddened when one of my newly ordained students found herself, in an online discussion with other Conservative rabbis, posing very nearly the same questions I asked shortly after my own ordination.

A paradox: does being part of the power structure of the Conservative movement mean I have to endorse others' power to deny me my power?

In order to continue thinking through power and its complexities, let me move now in a somewhat different direction. It is part of who I am and what I do that I should turn to rabbinic texts when confronted with difficult and/or pressing questions. So, what sources guide me, and what sources could I provide to my students to guide them in negotiating the many issues relating to power and its uses that they will encounter in their careers?

I think some of the most intriguing rabbinic discussions of power and leadership are stories rabbis tell about their own experiences serving as leaders of their communities. For example, the Rabbis tell us that one aspect of holding a position of leadership and power is that, inevitably, you will be challenged by those over whom you have authority—even from those who appointed you in the first place. The following brief story is from the Jerusalem Talmud, Pe'ah 8:6:

> They wanted to appoint R. Akiva as a community leader. He said to them, "Let me go consult with my household. They went after

him, and heard him saying, "Even though they will revile [me], even though they will curse [me]."

A somewhat similar story is told about Rabbi Elazar ben Azariah in the Babylonian Talmud, Berachot 27b–28a. In this episode, the Rabbis of the academy seek a new leader (and also tell us, by the way, some of the qualities they sought in a leader):

> They said, "Let us appoint Rabbi Elazar ben Azariah, for he is wise, and wealthy, and a 10th generation descendant of Ezra. . . . They came and said to him, "Would Master be willing to be the head of the academy?" He said to them, "I will go and consult with the members of my household." He went and consulted his wife. She said to him, "Perhaps they will (eventually) depose you?" He said to her, "Let a person use a precious vessel one day, and tomorrow let it be broken."

There is, however, another moral that I take out of both of these stories: the fact that I will meet with resistance to my power, resistance to my being in a position of leadership is not a good enough reason to refuse to exercise that power and that leadership. The vessel is indeed precious as well as fragile. If my purpose is to serve God and my community, then better to have used and valued the vessel than to never have held it at all. Better to share my title of rabbi with colleagues who are still not sure they want to share it with me, than to have failed to take the opportunity to do the work that I love.

Furthermore, when I move back a step or two and look at the larger context in which the story of Rabbi Elazar ben Azariah is found, I find yet more important teachings about the responsibilities of leaders and leadership. Rabbi Elazar ben Azariah is not only being asked to take a position of power but to replace Rabban Gamliel, who is not leaving his leadership role by choice. It is fairly clear as one reads the full story that in the eyes of the storyteller, Rabban Gamliel has repeatedly used his power and position to abuse one of his colleagues; thus the other Rabbis are justified in deposing him:

> Our rabbis taught: It once happened that a particular student came before Rabbi Yehoshua, and said to him, "Is (praying) the evening prayer service voluntary or obligatory?" He (Rabbi Yehoshua) said, "It is voluntary." He (the student) then came before Rabban Gamliel and said to him, "Is the evening prayer service voluntary or obligatory?" He (Rabban Gamliel) said, "It is obligatory." He (the student)

said, "But Rabbi Yehoshua told me that it is voluntary!" He (Rabban Gamliel) said to him, "Wait until the 'shield bearers' (i.e., the scholars) enter the study hall." When the 'shield bearers' entered, the inquirer stood and asked, "Is the evening prayer service voluntary or obligatory?" Rabban Gamliel said, "It is obligatory." Rabban Gamliel said to the sages, "Is there any one who disagrees in this matter?" Rabbi Yehoshua said to him, "No." He (Rabban Gamliel) said to him, "But it was reported to me in your name that it is voluntary!" He (Rabban Gamliel) said to him, "Yehoshua, stand up on your feet and let them testify against you. . . ." Rabban Gamliel was sitting and lecturing, and Rabbi Yehoshua stood on his feet, until all the people murmured. . . . They said, "How long will he (Rabban Gamliel) continue shaming Rabbi Yehoshua? He shamed him last year at Rosh Hashanah (see below); he shamed him regarding first-born animals, in the case of Rabbi Tzadok (Bechorot 36a). Come, let us depose him!"

Further on, other charges are brought against Rabban Gamliel: he limits access to the study hall and excludes people who genuinely want to learn, he is unaware of the difficult financial conditions under which many scholars live so as to be able to study, he has servants he may call on to impose his will on others. The example of Rabban Gamliel is therefore a reminder to me that having been allowed access to a certain kind of power and leadership in the Jewish community, I must always strive to use it ethically and with the ideal of serving the community. As a leader, I must always walk the fine line between being true to my convictions and/or community norms while striving to minimize the possibility of shutting out people who might want to participate or have something to contribute.

And finally, to be fair to Rabban Gamliel (and to add a level of complication to matters), let me relate one more story, the story of how Rabban Gamliel "shamed" Rabbi Yehoshua one year at Rosh Hashanah (Mishnah Rosh Hashanah 2:8–9). The story begins when Rabban Gamliel accepts testimony regarding the appearance of the new moon to determine the beginning of the new month. Doubt, however, is cast on the witnesses' report, and Rabbi Yehoshua sides with those questioning Rabban Gamliel's decision. Rabbi Yehoshua thus believes that Yom Kippur will take place a day later than it would according to Rabban Gamliel:

Rabban Gamliel sent to him (Rabbi Yehoshua): "I decree for you that you should come to me with your staff and your money on (the day that is) Yom Kippur by your calculations."

Rabbinic law forbids carrying these items on Yom Kippur. Since the day in question is, according to Rabban Gamliel, the day *after* Yom Kippur and a perfectly ordinary day, he is demanding that Rabbi Yehoshua also treat it as such, that he visibly demonstrate his acceptance of Rabban Gamliel's ruling.

> Rabbi Akiva went and found him (Rabbi Yehoshua) in distress. He (Rabbi Akiva) said to him, "I can demonstrate that everything that Rabban Gamliel has done is done (i.e., must be accepted as legally binding). . . . He (Rabbi Yehoshua) went to Rabbi Dosa ben Harkinus (who raised the initial objections to Rabban Gamliel's ruling!), and he (Rabbi Dosa) said to him, "If we are going to reconsider the rulings of Rabban Gamliel's court, then we must reconsider the rulings of every court from the days of Moses until now. . . . Rather, any three (judges) who arose over Israel as a court are like (as authoritative as) the court of Moses." He (Rabbi Yehoshua) took his staff and his money in his hand and went to Yavneh, to Rabban Gamliel, on the day that was Yom Kippur by his calculations. Rabban Gamliel stood and kissed him on his head, and said, "Come in peace, my master and my disciple; 'my master' in wisdom, and 'my disciple' in that you have accepted my words."

What I see in this story is that although Rabban Gamliel appears to act harshly toward Rabbi Yehoshua, he does so with a purpose, a purpose that eventually even Rabbi Yehoshua himself accepts and respects. That is, the community needs recognized sources of power and authority to function. Without them, the result is not freedom or autonomy, but anarchy.

As in many things, I find that the rabbinic evidence ends up counseling me in something like a "golden mean." I should not be afraid to work for a position of leadership out of fear of the resistance I might meet or the possibility that someone will challenge my right to a position of authority. The community needs leaders committed to its welfare. But if having achieved a position of leadership I fail to use my role for the benefit of the community—if I use it to shame or harm or arbitrarily exclude others—*then* it is good and right that others should resist my abuse of power. For the system to work, allowing necessary decisions to be made yet preventing abuses, power must always be balanced between those who are in positions to exercise it, and those who have granted it to them.

The Complex Power of a Rabbi

Laura Geller

W HEN I identify myself as rabbi, people return my phone calls. In the early part of my career, people on the other end of the phone assumed that I was the secretary who was going to leave a message for Rabbi Geller, but the calls still got returned. That's a kind of power: the rabbi as a person of stature is to be respected.

People tend not to curse in my presence and are a little bit careful about telling or forwarding me off-color jokes. That's a kind of power: the rabbi as a *kli kodesh,* a "holy instrument," must apparently not be tarnished by inappropriate words.

When they are in the hospital, congregants want me to visit, expect me to visit, and want me to speak their names when we offer the prayer for healing during services. That's a kind of power: the rabbi is a surrogate for the community and for God. As much as I have tried to create a culture in which congregants take care of each other during times of illness or crisis or loss, people still want to see their rabbi as God's personal representative, even those who claim not to believe in God.

It's a little more complicated with women rabbis, since most Jews still carry within themselves a childlike conception of God as a being with a male gender. This misconception emerges most starkly at moments of crisis when the "normal" order of life is disrupted by forces beyond our control . . . by "God." The rabbi, as supposedly being "closer to God" or "invested by God" or "called by God," naturally becomes God's stand-in. When the rabbi is a man, especially an older man with a resonant voice, the transference happens without the individual even being aware of it. When the rabbi is a woman, the transference is blocked. Sometimes the disconnect challenges the individual to stop and reflect on how he or she thinks about God. (This is part of the reason there has been such a revolution in Jewish thought about theology, spirituality, and reenvisioning liturgy over the past thirty years since the ordination of women.)

This kind of symbolic power is problematic at best and dangerous at worst. It is problematic because no rabbi can be there all the time for the entire community, so someone is always going to be disappointed or hurt. It makes community building difficult because congregants depend on the rabbi and not on each other. And the message it sends about Judaism is wrong: the tradition is quite clear that visiting the sick or comforting the mourner is a mitzvah incumbent on *each* Jew, not the special domain of the rabbi. It is one more example of how contemporary liberal Judaism has enabled the rabbi to "be Jewish" for the rest of the congregation. The rabbi has been given symbolic power, while the individuals in the community have allowed themselves to be disempowered.

Symbolic power can also be dangerous. Boundary violations involving rabbis can happen when rabbis use their symbolic power in an abusive way. Rabbis are not God, nor are they any more God's representative than anyone else. When transference occurs, however, the congregant is particularly vulnerable to inappropriate attention and intimacy. And unfortunately, some rabbis take advantage of that vulnerability.

Because transference of this kind is less likely to happen when the rabbi is a woman, women rabbis are in a unique position to help congregants think differently about the power of the rabbi. This was made most clear to me in two conversations that took place immediately after I finished leading my first High Holy Day services. A woman came up to me with great excitement: "Rabbi, these were the most meaningful High Holy Day services I have ever experienced! I realized that if you could be a rabbi, then I could be a rabbi, and if I could be a rabbi, then I can take responsibility for my own Jewish life." Seconds later a man came over with a slightly different nuance: "Rabbi, I realized that if you can be a rabbi, then *certainly* I can be a rabbi . . . and so I can take responsibility for my own Jewish life." Even now, thirty years later, people still attribute less authority to women than to men. Instead of viewing this as a problem, it might actually be an opportunity for women rabbis to teach the Jewish community that individuals are in fact responsible for their own Jewish lives and ought to notice when they give that power away.

Still, there is transference of a different kind with women rabbis. Some congregants want me to be the all-forgiving and embracing mother they never had and become outraged when I disappoint them. One example occurred soon after I arrived at the congregation. A woman came to see me to complain that I would not have officiated at her daughter's wedding. The daughter had married a religious Christian several years before and although she had found a rabbi to do the service, it infuriated her that her rabbi would not have officiated. As we talked, I explained to her that if this were my daughter, I would be there as a mom, but I couldn't be there as a rabbi. Her response was telling: "But as a rabbi you are a mother to us . . . and you have to support us no matter what we do."

This is power, but it is not the kind of power I want.

The power that I want is to empower my congregants to be more thoughtful Jews and more engaged human beings. I want to help them discover that Judaism can make a difference in their lives and can strengthen their commitments to make a difference in the world. I try to do that in several ways. First, I try to model through my own life what one version of a committed Jewish life looks like. I take my inner life very seriously, and my congregants know that. I pray regularly; and even when I am not leading services, I am a congregant in my synagogue. Congregants know that I have been moving in a spiritual direction for many years now because I speak about the experience in sermons and write about it in newsletter columns. They know that I have a regular practice of meditation and that I have participated in silent meditation retreats. They know I continue to study, not just to prepare for classes and sermons. They have supported my learning at the Hartman Institute in Jerusalem as well as in various study partnerships over the years. And they know of my involvement in social justice issues, locally, nationally, and in Israel. So I would hope that my power comes from modeling one version of an authentic Jewish life, in which prayer, learning, and social justice are at the center.

Second, I hope my power comes from my learning and teaching. This kind of power is quite different from the traditional power of the rabbi to tell his congregants what to do in a particular situation involving ritual or ethical concerns. In general, my congregation, like most Reform congregations, is not particularly interested in matters of ritual or Jewish law. But there are certain ethical decisions over which they sometimes do turn to their rabbi, particularly around beginning- and end-of-life issues: infertility, abortion, and questions around caring for a loved one with a terminal illness. My power, in these counseling situations, flows from my Jewish learning as well as from my ability to help them apply the insights of Jewish tradition to the decisions they have to make. I don't make the decisions as a traditional rabbi may have, but rather I empower congregants to make their own decisions based on Jewish values.

Third, my power comes from finding partners who share my vision for the synagogue. Although I do not technically hire or fire senior staff members, it would be extremely unlikely that anyone would be selected if I were not his or her advocate. So over the years I have been able to assemble a team of talented professionals who are genuine colleagues. Ours is not a hierarchal model in which the senior rabbi makes the decisions that are then implemented by the staff, but rather a web model in which we work in teams, collaborate on joint projects, and at the same time follow our own individual passions, implementing new ideas and not being afraid to take risks or even to fail. I share my power with my colleagues, many of whom I have worked with for over 10 years.

I also share power with the lay people who are my partners. The board of directors is my boss, yet I have real input into who those directors should be. As a board, we study together, plan together, and reflect on the challenges and successes of the synagogue together.

When I think about the nature of power in my rabbinate, I don't aspire to be a Moses. I don't want to be the symbolic exemplar who lifts up his arms and parts the seas. I don't have the talent to be the powerful orator who moved his community through the words of Devarim. I am not an Aaron whose technical skill with ritual can effectuate atonement for his community. I am not brave enough to be an Isaiah challenging my community to live up to its best version of itself. Instead, I aspire to be more like Ruth and more like Deborah. Like Ruth, I would welcome the power that comes from living a life of *hesed,* of touching people in gentle ways, helping them discover compassion in themselves and bringing them to work together. And like Deborah, I hope that my learning and my spiritual work give me the clarity that she had sitting under her tamarisk tree, enabling her to see clearly as she taught and advised people who came to her for counsel. And like Deborah, I hope I am a partner to those in the congregation who, like Barak, have different skills from mine but who, by working together, can achieve a vision of a congregation that makes a difference in people's lives. Deborah is called "Eishet Lappidoth," usually translated as "the wife of Lappidoth." But "lappidoth" comes from the word meaning "wicks" or "torches." So perhaps this appellation, "woman of torches," is the secret to her power and leadership: she is the one who lights the torches of other people, and together with them, creates a greater, more illuminating light. This is the power to which I aspire.

The Power of Ideals

Personhood and Power

James S. Diamond

W HAT IS power? To be understood in any meaningful way, power needs a context in which it can be seen to operate. There are many contexts in which power can be observed. The kind of power I want to talk about is illustrated in the following story.

During the Holocaust a group of Hasidim, men, women, and children, were rounded up by the SS and then led to the edge of a wooded ravine. They knew what awaited them: they would be stripped naked and shot by a troop of Einsatzgruppen commandos. When they arrived at the killing ground, before they began to disrobe, the leader of the group, their rebbe, asked the Sonderkommandant if he and his troops could wait a few minutes before beginning the shooting. The rebbe wanted to prepare his community for their imminent martyrdom. The Sonderkommandant readily agreed; what difference would a few minutes make?

The rebbe then assembled his weeping charges near the edge of the pit. He told them that just as they had been bidden to love and serve God in life, so now were they being given the chance to do so in leaving this world. He then led them in a special *nigun,* one of the haunting wordless melodies Hasidim sing. Higher and higher their voices rose. Then, vigorously and in unison, they all said the *Shema.* Then the rebbe said to the Sonderkommandant, "We are ready; you may begin."

The Sonderkommandant gave the order. But there was no shooting. The German commandos couldn't pull the triggers. They had been totally unnerved by what they had seen. It took the consumption of several bottles of liquor and the screamed threats by the Sonderkommandant that the nonshooters would themselves be executed before the machine guns barked into operation.[1]

---

1. I heard this story many years ago from Rabbi Yitz Greenberg. I have checked with him about its source, but it is unknown to him now. He remembers clearly the first two paragraphs but is not certain about the third one as I have related it. I take my cue here

This story, whatever else it tells us, is about power and how it can be used. But it is power of a different order from that of armies and political leaders. Over against the power of the Sonderkommandant is the power of the rebbe. Over against the guns of the Nazi soldiers positioned at the pit was the existential energy that permeated the collective presence of the men, women, and children who huddled at its edge. I would call this existential energy spiritual power. As a manifestation of power, it is less obvious and less tangible than brute force or financial clout or racial and gender dominance. This kind of power operates more subtly. Yet as we see in this story, it is every bit as palpable and as consequential.

The Bible knows about these two qualitatively different modes of power. It uses two different Hebrew words to denote them. Consider this passage from the book of Deuteronomy, the fifth of the five books of Moses: "When you have eaten your fill, and have built fine houses to live in, and your herds and flocks have multiplied, and your silver and gold have increased, and everything you own has prospered, beware lest your heart grow haughty and you forget the Lord your God . . . and you say to yourselves, 'My own power (*kohi*) and the might of my own hand have won this wealth for me'" (Deuteronomy 8:12–17). Compare that with these oft-cited verses from the prophet Zechariah, "Not by might, nor by power (*koach*), but by My spirit (*ruach*)—said the Lord of Hosts" (Zechariah 4:6), and from the very end of Psalm 29, "May the Lord grant strength (*oz*) to His people; may the Lord bestow on His people wellbeing" (Psalms 29:11.)

Koach is physically or socially determined, deriving from such externalities as physique, title, rank, and class. *Ruach* and *oz,* on the other hand, originate within. Power that is socially or externally defined is acquired in any number of ways: through training, education, and experience; by appointment, connections, pedigree, and conspiracy; and so on. (I am not equating these means.) Existential or spiritual power comes from a very different source.

Such power—internal and individual—accrues to us from our personhood. Or perhaps it is the other way around: our personhood is innately imbued with power. We may not always know this. We may not always be conscious of it. Sometimes we feel as if we had no power. The world and society often conspire to make us feel powerless. But the happy secret

---

from what Elie Wiesel once wrote: "Some events do take place but are not true; others are—although they never occurred" (Introduction to *Legends of Our Time* [New York: Holt, Rinehart & Winston, 1968], viii).

about each of us is that we are not impotent. No matter who or where we are in the scheme of things, whether teacher or student, employee or CEO, parent or child, senator or voting citizen, congregant or rabbi, patient or doctor, therapist or counselee, salesperson or customer, even prisoner or captor—we have power. We can act. Or react. True, the quality and quantity of our power may in some situations be limited, but it is there if we know how to locate it and how to use it.

How do we use it? How do we actualize in our daily life this power that accrues from our personhood? I see three ways in which we leverage it as we go through this world: authority, influence, and responsibility.

Authority

Power confers authority. But just as there are different kinds of power, so are there different kinds of authority. Social, or what I've called "external," power confers social or external authority. In the case of the Hasidim, there was no question who was ultimately in charge and who would set the rules. In a conflict between labor and management the reality is that the boss may not always be right, but he or she is always the boss. That's external authority.

Internal authority is something different. It is determined by the persona, that ineffable aura that emanates from a person when that person communicates his or her very personhood. What is this aura? It was what enabled Natan Sharansky to withstand the external power the KGB wielded over him. It was what caused the rebbe and his community to freeze the trigger fingers of the SS gunmen. It was internal, existential, spiritual power.

Influence

Closely related to authority, but not quite the same thing, is influence. Perhaps influence is one kind of authority or an aspect of it. But power does include influence. What else enabled the rebbe to persuade the Sonderkommandant to give him those few minutes? What was it that enabled the Hasidim to follow the rebbe in the first place and to accept what he was doing with them? One of the remarkable things about internal power is that while it cannot undo the imbalance of external power in a relationship, it still can endow the one who is manifestly weaker with a measure of moral influence.

Responsibility

Power of whatever kind cannot be wielded indiscriminately. In fact, there may be an inverse ratio between power and its exercise. The more expended, the less effective it becomes. Which argues for the idea that the more power one has, the less it needs to be or should be used. The questions then become: when do I consciously use my power? And how? This is when the issue of responsibility comes in: to whom I am responsible? In his situation, the rebbe understood that he had a responsibility not only to his Hasidim but to himself and to the whole tradition he embodied. That is what emboldened him to ask for time and thus change the whole dynamic between the murderers and the victims. And maybe it went further than that: maybe the rebbe used his power in that extreme situation because at that moment he saw the SS men not as anonymous killers but as fellow human beings, and he felt some responsibility even to them. His internal power empowered them to access their own and served to remind them, at least for a few minutes, that they, too, were human beings. The whole exchange was transformative.

Such internal or spiritual power, *ruach* and *oz,* does not come easily to us. It may be a function of our very personhood, but it is not activated and developed without hard inner work. To acquire this kind of power we need to develop our inner musculature in the same way weight lifters or wrestlers develop their biceps and pectorals. Different people will do this in different ways. They will access this power according to the beliefs and assumptions with which they meet the world. The religionist, for whom God is a reality, however elusive and inscrutable, has a power source to plug into. When you understand yourself as a spark off the divine anvil, you connect your being to a cosmic energy flow and thereby fill it with clarity, direction, and meaning. The secularist will empower himself or herself in this way differently. For when God and religious language are problematical, or are out of the question altogether, you ascend not to a transcendental realm that is unfathomable to you but rather you go deep inside yourself, until you locate what you know to be the power source at the ground of your own being. In either case, though, the outcome of such inner work is the same: the ability to say to yourself "I know who I am and I know what I stand for. I know what I would die for and I—therefore—know what I am living for." These are the indicators of the kind of power that *ruach* and *oz* supply. They imbue us with what the Protestant thinker Paul Tillich called "the courage to be." That is what the rebbe and his community achieved before they died, and that is what I believe each of us can achieve while we are privileged to be here in this life.

The Privilege to Choose, the Power to Change
Zachary Lazarus

E VERY DAY I open a newspaper and read about another tragedy. A cadre of cronies run the place that we call America, Home of the Free. Name an issue: political corruption, torture, genocide, public school systems, the environment, dependency on fossil fuel, women's right to choose, the devaluation and degradation of an individual's rights, health care, Social Security, the aftermath of Hurricane Katrina, and the list of tragedies continues. If *"freedom'*s just another word for nothing left to lose," many Americans, and citizens of the world, are not too far off. We might gain our freedom still.

As a senior at Wesleyan University, a school well known for its political activism, I spent spring break in 2005 volunteering in the Ninth Ward in New Orleans. I traveled with a group of five other Jewish students, all devoted to expressing their religion through their commitment to social justice. We worked with the Common Ground Collective, alongside over a 1,000 students who all volunteered their spring breaks. Wesleyan sent 75 students to the organization, one of the highest turnouts among all of the schools represented.

I came to Wesleyan thrilled to be engulfed by political struggles and conversations and to finally develop a Jewish community of my own. At school, the Jewish community challenged and supported me, shook my assumptions, danced and sang with me. At school I did my first volunteer work trip with Habitat for Humanity during spring break my freshman year. Later, through the Jewish community, I attended a mostly Northeastern Jewish retreat called Fruity Jews in the Woods. It's an informal, pluralist spiritual weekend with lots of song and dance.

Through connections from that retreat and from Wesleyan, I gathered a group to register voters in Seattle during the summer of 2004. Senior year, during winter break, I went to Biloxi, Mississippi, through a Hillel volunteer trip. My spring break senior year, the same group who worked with Hillel went on our own to New Orleans. That trip remains the highlight of all of my experiences in college. Intimate retellings of the sights and stories still bring tears to my eyes.

The area looked disastrous: city hall in shambles; high-rises still requiring repair; houses full of mold from floor to ceiling; and, in the Ninth Ward, houses on top of cars, houses in the middle of the street, empty lots where houses once existed. A lot full of small, temporary buildings served as a police station. Close to the Industrial Canal in the Ninth Ward, where several levees broke, only a slab of concrete remained, with an address hurriedly spray-painted as proof that the site was not abandoned. Residents who remained in the area often shared their tragic stories and expressed their misery and hope.

Their experiences disclose the extent to which racism, and not simply Mother Nature, transformed the Ninth Ward into the disaster zone that remained so seven months after the storm. People opened their hearts to us so that we could use their stories to help get them what they really need—not volunteers, but government support in rebuilding their lives. Our privileged status granted us access to a government that largely ignored these New Orleans residents. We were mostly white and upper-middle-class college students and could thus make our voices heard without the same degree of fear of repercussions.

We removed plaster covered in mold, distributed food and water, and helped people throw away nearly every item that they owned. We listened to the stories of residents who lost everything, who were forgotten by the government. Stories of three generations spread from one household to cities throughout the United States. Hope uncomfortably quelled residents' desperation and misery, the hope that visitors like us would go home and advocate for change; that future action might stem from our increased knowledge of the region's culture, history, and life; hope that they would not be forgotten, although to a large extent they already have been. We learned about life in particularly difficult circumstances and about the integral role hope plays in survival.

Upon return to Wesleyan, silence reigned on campus. No advocacy, no information, no public discussion. Eventually, a couple of small presentations were given, and an educational display was set up during finals week. This fallout was not unique. The lackluster political scene extended to nearly all realms of campus. On campus and beyond, nihilism thrives because change seems impossible. We watch Jon Stewart and laugh, and maybe cry, as we mumble to ourselves about the sorry state of the world. The voter turnout rate of the 2004 election was 64 percent of the eligible populace. Generation Y's voting rate was 47 percent, lower than any other demographic.[1]

---

1. According to the U.S. Census Bureau, May 26, 2005, available at www.census.gov/ Press-Release/www/releases/archives/voting/004986.html.

Energy for creating change is fragmented at best. We learn how to critique and deconstruct, but we often refuse to create anything ourselves. When this tendency is taken to extremes, it can become ironically destructive. While working at one of Common Ground's distribution centers in the Ninth Ward, a largely African American community, I met a handful of young white couples who had recently moved to New Orleans. They intended to buy dirt-cheap real estate and start a punk commune. Striving to live outside "the system," they found a place where it has almost entirely fallen apart.

The result: residents now share scarce, often donated, resources with people disconnected from Katrina's tragedy. Taking advantage of a dire situation, these disaffected youth only reinforce the difference between the haves and the have-nots in this world. The system that so many of my generation want to live beyond understands this rejection as a form of submission. Political silence often becomes tacit consent for the maintenance of the status quo. Unorganized withdrawal does not create change. In New Orleans, while these alienated youth transcend the system, they also burden those most denigrated by it.

Registering voters in Seattle during the summer of 2004, I heard similar nihilistic attitudes. The most frequent reason for refusing to register to vote was, "My vote doesn't count." Dissatisfaction with corrupt politicians who wouldn't make a difference led to political withdrawal. Making an individual choice not to vote may have symbolic meaning, but without a movement, without organizing, such a choice just grants elected politicians political immunity. Our politicians should work for us, but we are responsible for holding them accountable. Our votes should declare the state of our satisfaction with our government. Dissatisfaction with political options could lead to an organized boycott of elections or to a write-in campaign. We must tell politicians or political parties why we refuse to vote so that our complaints will create change.

We, the white Jewish upper-middle class who grew up in the plentiful 1990s, have not had to fight for our liberties. No draft forces us onto the battlefield and, two generations removed from the Holocaust, Hillel and Jewish studies departments thrive like never before. We get to decide the degree to which we assimilate, the degree to which we relate to our tradition, and the degree to which we act on our beliefs. These are privileges.

Political nihilism stems from these privileges. Those who suffer cannot choose to ignore their suffering. Residents of the Ninth Ward live as they must, striving to survive, working to gain a semblance of normalcy after Katrina. I write this essay in part because I see the nihilist impulses in myself, and I don't want them to prevail.

Parents in the lower Ninth Ward have organized. Tired of eight months of deafening silence regarding the opening of the public school system, they asked Common Ground to gut Martin Luther King Jr. Elementary. Gutting the school was illegal because the state was paying a private contractor to rebuild the school district, but the residents were willing to take that risk. The corporation had sat on its hands for months. Not a single school had been touched. The residents had nothing left to lose. Their neighborhood was in shambles, and without basic social services it would remain that way.

Every house in the Ninth Ward needed gutting: disposal of furniture, toys, photos, counters, and plaster. Sitting water as high as 18 feet mangled everything but the frames of the houses still standing. The number of bodies found on the premises remains brightly spray-painted on every house.

While countless Americans fight for basic social services, we, the privileged, complain that our voices don't count. We say that we cannot make a real difference anyway. We choose to opt out of politics without self-reflection. When we do not stand up for our beliefs, we insult those who have to. Our withdrawal from politics, in effect, becomes tacit consent for the status quo.

Instead of allowing discontent to immobilize us, we must harness our discontent. We must foster the ability to think strategically. Change comes from community and conversations, creativity and personal expression. Change comes from individuals' acts and a connection to one's roots. Change comes from the intersection of knowledge, sweat, and poetry. We must reclaim belief. There's a link between my disaffected impulses and alienation from my religious tradition.

My Judaism is integral to my own activism; my background, my belief, my ritual, and my community give me reasons to fight. They make me accountable and support me in my discomfort. My Jewish community opens interfaith conversations, and it sustains me as I enact my values.

Both in Seattle and on the Gulf Coast I worked with spiritual Jewish communities that granted me hope in the face of destruction. These individuals facilitated conversation, encouraged creativity, and nourished me in my desperation and helplessness upon seeing tragedy.

For me, that nourishment extends beyond the Jewish community. Jewish texts contain any number of thoughts, struggles, and theologies. I don't embrace every law without critique, but neither do I dismiss traditional texts outright. I am not advocating for any particular approach to Judaism, nor do I think that all of our answers lie in ancient works foreign to contemporary feminist criticisms. I do believe that all of us would gain from a commitment to some sort of Jewishness. Meaning and commitment, although often dictated by dire need, can stem from tradition as well. I particularly enjoy studying with my text study partner, my *hevruta.* Conversation creates community, creates change.

One text that I find particularly inspiring is the *Kedushat Levi.* It was written by Rabbi Levi Yitzchak of Berditchev, an important 18th-century Hasidic rabbi. The book contains his own commentary on the entire Torah. In his discussion of the parashah (Torah portion) Metsora, the rabbi addressed the problem of anthropomorphisms in our texts. If God is incorporeal, how can so much of the Torah, our most direct link to the divine, describe God's human traits? Although I do not accept the concept that the Torah is infallible, the rabbi's response remains inspiring.

The heavens, Rabbi Yitzchak wrote, are expressed in our actions. Just as your shadow reflects your movements on earth, when you see justly, you see as God's eyes see in the heavens. When you hear with justice, you render God's ears. Each individual's actions create and empower that individual's connection to the divine. I understand the rabbi to be saying that we create God not through dogma but through our deeds.

Belief, whether in a divinity or a political ideology, can motivate us to enact our ideals in the face of nihilism. Contemporary thinkers, theological and not, offer plenty of tools for empowerment. However, we must invest ourselves in the process of creating change for these tools to have value. I enjoy Saul Alinsky's *Rules for Radicals* and love Abraham Joshua Heschel's *The Prophets,* but both texts are flat without the commitment to engage them with our own hearts, minds, and bodies.

Today's ethical questions for those of us disaffected by our government include these: Should we engage? Can we make change? Will we try? Some of us even pretend to live beyond the confines of the government. Cynically watching Jon Stewart while denying our own power to create change is one choice. It's an easy choice because we won't fail if we don't try.

Instead, we can choose to act on our politics. We can act on the knowledge that our everyday acts, from what car we drive to how we treat those around us no matter their social stature, are political and moral decisions. We must reclaim the notion that we can make a difference. Organizations such as MoveOn.org, American Jewish World Service,

People for the American Way, StandNow.org, PIRG, and Citizen Action *are* making a difference.

Governor Christine Gregoire won Washington State's 2004 gubernatorial election by less than 200 votes. My friends and I registered 7,000 people; our work in Washington mattered. The organization we worked with registered over 40,000. Nothing guarantees success, but inaction guarantees failure. Our success in Washington occurred because a few college students, with a free summer break, made a commitment. We voiced our opinions through our actions and helped make real change.

I believe that we make God through our acts, that our abilities to create echo God's Creation and that my Judaism and my commitment to social justice are one. That is what keeps me motivated, even as I doubt my abilities to help rebuild New Orleans while attending a private, elite college in Connecticut.

Countless people have not been welcome to open shop, join a club, immigrate, pray, or move into a particular neighborhood. Maybe one of those people was a grandparent of yours who fled Europe during World War II. Fighting for our ideals is an option; we can also choose to try opting out of the world around us. That is true privilege, the freedom of choice.

Let's do something radical, something extraordinary. Let's force the politicians who claim to represent us to actually represent us. Let's cast off our yokes of being fed up and join with those who are fed up but are willing to do something about it. There are plenty of us who *do* act on our ideals. Let's all join them.

Consider all of the opportunities that you have had to succeed. How did those come to you? At whose expense? Have you ever thrived on the losses of others, like those who moved to New Orleans to live outside the system? We all have. Are those young people really so different from any of us? Was my inaction after my trip to New Orleans so different from the youth who moved to the Ninth Ward to take the easy way out?

There's a famous Rabbinic saying in the Mishnah (Avot 2:16): "You are not required to complete the work, but neither are you free to desist from it." I know that together, through community, through commitment and constant struggle we can make a difference. I know that because it has happened, it is happening right now, and I have been a part of its happening. Ideals can become a reality; we just need a little faith and a lot of each other.

PART III

CONCLUSION

The Ethics of Power

The Many Forms of Power

E ACH OF us, in one way or another, exercises power over others. By the same token, each of us is subject to the power of others. At the most basic level, each of us has the power to hurt and be hurt through our physical and verbal interactions with one another every day. But in far more complex and subtle ways, we also exercise power by virtue of our status, our money, our positions of authority, our knowledge, and a host of other personal qualities and circumstances. Indeed, every social relationship in some fashion involves exercising power vis-à-vis others, and thus every relationship involves questions of ethics. The use of power is so basic to our lives and so inextricably bound up with moral choices that perhaps no subject is more fraught with moral significance than the use of power.

The ways in which this is so will become evident as we explore the nature of power—the many forms of power, the ways in which it is acquired and exercised, and the diverse purposes for which it is used. We can begin to get a handle on these complex matters by considering a few basic realities.

Having power is not an all-or-nothing affair. Many people exercise power in some aspects of their lives, but not in others. The CEO exerts power over her employees but is subject to the power of state regulations and the officials who make and enforce them. The parent exerts power over his children, but is subject to the power of his employer, his rabbi (or other religious leader), and his physician, among many others. Even the president of the United States can be voted out of office or impeached, and his veto can be overridden. It follows that no one is absolutely powerful or absolutely powerless.

Moreover, the degree to which one possesses power is rather fluid. Every parent knows that she has a great deal of power over her children when they are very young and far less as they grow up and become more independent. And even at the same stage in life, the degree of one's power over others can fluctuate from day to day, depending on the particular tenor and circumstances of one's interactions—just ask the parent of any two-year-old! We all know of situations, too, in which someone with a great deal of power, such as a politician, loses it through a failure (or even a perceived failure) to use that power wisely or legally.

Finally, having power and being aware of having it are two quite different things. In many situations, people feel disempowered when, in fact, they have unrealized opportunities to challenge those in power or even to seize it for themselves. Workers who organize a union to demand certain benefits from their employers, African Americans who march nonviolently to demand their rights from racist (or apathetic) politicians, even seniors who order their prescription drugs from Canada to challenge the high prices the pharmaceutical companies charge in the United States—all these are examples of people who might appear to be lacking in power but who actually use their latent power very effectively. Even concentration camp inmates, who would seem to have been utterly stripped of their power by the Nazis and their collaborators, could exercise a certain kind of power. Victor Frankl shows in his famous book *Man's Search for Meaning* that inmates had the power to believe that their lives had meaning and, in so doing, to transcend their suffering and improve their chances of survival. As he wrote, this is a kind of power that defines our humanity and that can never be taken away from us, no matter how dehumanized we have been by those who wield power over us.

So, we may ask, what *is* power? How shall we analyze the moral issues that arise in connection with using (or not using) one's power? In the most general sense, power is the ability to do something, to actualize one's desires and wishes, to act on one's intentions, beliefs, and feelings. I have physical power if I can get from point A to point B or if I can put something together or take it apart, as I choose. In this sense, power is simply freedom—to decide and then to act on that decision.

But the most interesting aspects of power arise in the context of our relationships with others, for it is here that we face others with their own will and their own freedom to actualize their desires. Now our freedom and our power are constrained in some measure by the ability of others to respond to our use of power. Consider any relationship in which one party exercises power over another and you will immediately realize how complex the dynamics of power become. The politician exercises power over his constituents, who also exercise the power to vote him out of office; the corporation exercises power in the marketplace but is also subject to the power of consumers through their preferences, perceptions, and buying power; the teacher exercises power over her students, but is also constrained by the ability of those students to grant or withhold their cooperation and approval. Moreover, having power and having a legitimate claim to that power can be quite different, as we know from the case of dictators who seize power in military coups.

The Morality of Power: Its Source, Goals, and Means

This is precisely where the interesting and unavoidable moral issues arise. For the one thing that power cannot do is secure its own legitimacy; in the words of the time-honored aphorism, "Might does not make right." What does make power "right" is a complex and disputed issue, which we can best understand by first considering the three dimensions of power: its source, its goals, and its means.

People reach positions of power in different ways and by virtue of different attributes. Professionals are powerful by virtue of their specialized knowledge and training, managers are powerful by virtue of their place within a corporate hierarchy, some leaders are powerful by virtue of their personal charisma, police officers and judges are powerful by virtue of the role they play within a much larger system of legal authorities. When we consider the *source* of one's power, we are asking, What gives this individual a particular set of freedoms and abilities that constitute his or her power over others?

Power is always exercised with some *goal* or purpose in mind. Teachers and parents ideally use their positions of power to inform, motivate, and nurture those for whom they are responsible. Groups of workers may use their power to strike as a way to achieve certain benefits to which they feel entitled. Religious leaders may use their power to inspire their congregants to live lives of greater religious devotion. In all these cases, powerful people use their power to achieve certain ends, often to influence or change other people or social conditions. Needless to say, because no one has complete control over any social interaction, it often happens that people who exercise power fail to achieve their intended goals.

Finally, people in positions of power generally have more than one *means* by which to wield that power in pursuit of their goals. Thus a classroom teacher can help a student be more diligent and learn more by offering extra credit for extra work, by spending time tutoring her, by giving her praise for work well done (or failing grades for work poorly done), and by calling on her parents and others to provide additional encouragement, among many other strategies. Some of these strategies may be more effective and/or prudent than others, but all are legitimate insofar as they fall within the powers that the teacher has by virtue of his position.

Noticing these dimensions of power helps us see the different ways in which the exercise of power can be moral or immoral. At each point—with respect to source, goals, or means—the use of power can be called into question on moral grounds. As we already noted, political power may be acquired immorally through the sheer exercise of military force or morally through the consent of the governed, as in the case of free and fair elections. A professional, such as a physician, may use her power to benefit her patients or to line her pockets by fraudulently billing the Medicare system. A corporate executive may use his legitimate power to promote others within the organization either by following established procedures for rewarding excellent job performance or in exchange for sexual favors. In each of these cases, moral considerations come into play with respect to the source, goals, or means of exercising power.

Can we say anything in general about what defines the moral use of power?

In response to this question, some ethicists (especially those in the tradition of John Locke and Immanuel Kant) would point to the notion of rights. Individuals (and, some would argue, groups as well) have basic rights that may not be violated by those who exercise power over them. And if those rights are violated, people may have the right to resist, to receive compensation, and/or to appeal to a higher authority to halt the abuse of power. We are most familiar with the idea of rights within the political sphere, especially the key role that this concept plays in American democracy, as enshrined in the words of the Declaration of Independence: "We hold these truths to be self-evident, that all men are created equal, that they are endowed by their Creator with certain unalienable rights, that among these are life, liberty and the pursuit of happiness." On this view, God has created us as free and independent creatures, who have the intrinsic right to use that freedom to pursue the goods essential to human life, as we see fit. This fundamental right acts as a constraint on the ways in which others can exercise power over us.

Classical Jewish teachings on the use of power tend to focus more on "obligations" than on rights, though the extent to which this is substantively different is a matter of some debate. Biblical sources do not invoke the rights of all people in society to certain essential goods but instead emphasize the obligation of all to care for those who are needy and marginalized. Similarly, Rabbinic discussions of criminal procedure stress the obligations of witnesses and judges, not the rights of defendants. Despite these differences, the main point is that the exercise of power must be constrained by a consideration for those affected by it. What distinguishes the moral use of power from brute force is that the former always takes into account some principle—the rights of the other, certain virtues that we must strive to embody, or a particular vision of a just society—in terms of which the exercise of power may be judged to be either moral or immoral. We can see the various ways in which such constraints might work in practice by exploring one of the case studies presented in Part I in somewhat more detail.

The second case study involved a rabbi, Larry, who is friends with a congregant, Neil. Larry reveals to Neil that he views Internet pornography with some frequency. Before turning to the questions of Neil's responsibility to report the rabbi's behavior to members of the synagogue's board of directors, let us consider the possible permutations of this case. Suppose that during his interview Larry had been asked specifically about his use of the Internet or, even more specifically, about whether he ever uses the Internet to view pornography. (This may be implausible, but it is certainly within the realm of possibility, particularly if, let's suppose, an earlier rabbi had been dismissed for sexual improprieties.) If Larry had lied about this and so misrepresented his moral character as better than it is, one could reasonably conclude that he has acquired his current power as rabbi through (at least partly) illegitimate means. Were this fact to come to light, one could argue that the congregation has the right to exercise its power to terminate Larry's contract on the grounds that they would never have hired him in the first place if they had been aware of his behavior. (Consider, by analogy, the case of people who lie about their past misdeeds when applying to immigrate to this country and then face being stripped of their citizenship and deported when those facts are disclosed.) In short, Larry's "right" to his position as rabbi, with all the power and authority that it entails, is legitimate only insofar as he has not deceived others, depriving them of their right to know whom they are hiring.

We could extend this analysis to questions of the purpose or goals of exercising power. Neil has a certain power by virtue of knowing some untoward facts about Larry's behavior. He could use this power to urge Larry to seek counseling to address his problem, or to blackmail Larry into giving him some public honor in the synagogue, or to force Larry into giving him money in exchange for Neil's agreement not to disclose this information to others. In other words, Neil could use his power either to help Larry or to help himself, if he so chooses. Clearly, though, enriching himself through the power he wields over Larry would be outright extortion and thus morally unacceptable.

Finally, the means by which Neil uses his power also has moral repercussions. If we posit that Neil has tried and failed to convince Larry to give up his Internet habit or to seek help, he might well feel an obligation to make this information known to people in positions of authority within the synagogue. He could do this in several ways: by having a discreet, confidential conversation with the president of the congregation; by sneaking into Larry's office when he is not there, removing his computer, and turning it over to the president of the congregation; or by sending a mass e-mail message to the entire membership of the congregation revealing what he knows about Larry's behavior. Obviously, these are not morally equivalent ways of exercising his power and obligation to hold the rabbi accountable for his behavior.

These different scenarios highlight the fact that one's acquisition of power, as well as the purposes for which and the means by which one uses that power, may be more or less moral, depending on the extent to which the rights of others are respected. Even if in some sense one's goals are noble and legitimate, acquiring power through fraud or exercising it through extortion or character assassination is plainly immoral. At every point in Neil's interactions with Larry, moral questions arise about how he will use his power, what rights he has, and what obligations he has toward others.

Balancing Duties to Many Parties

This last point leads to another important observation about the ethics of power. Frequently, the exercise of power affects more than one group of people and so entails the balancing of competing sets of obligations. This, too, can be illustrated using the case of Larry and Neil. In one sense, Neil has an obligation to protect Larry's dignity and privacy, despite the fact that he has engaged in behavior that many would regard as immoral. By the same token, Neil has an obligation to inform the congregation that its spiritual leader is someone whose moral character is questionable. At some point, Neil will have to engage in a difficult and imprecise moral deliberation about how each potential decision he makes will respect (or violate) these competing obligations. (Note that the same dilemma could be formulated using the language of liberalism in terms of competing rights— Larry's right to his privacy and the congregation's right to choose a rabbi whose moral judgment they trust.) Balancing such competing obligations (or rights) is always a matter of judgment that reasonable and morally sensitive people can (and often do) make in diverse ways.

Similar sorts of moral conflicts can be found in many other situations. Corporate CEOs have responsibilities to their shareholders but also to the employees of the company and to the members of the public who purchase their products; physicians have responsibilities to their patients as individuals but also to their employers and to their profession and even to the ideal of promoting public health. Many of our most vexing moral dilemmas arise precisely in situations of this sort, when the exercise of power brings with it the ability to affect the lives of many others as well as the responsibility to protect the rights of many others. In such situations, it is often tempting to simplify the problem by denying that one's actions have the claimed effect on others or by asserting that the action in question does not violate anyone's legitimate rights. We can all think of situations in which such claims are made, sometimes by people who are genuinely unable to see the moral dimensions of their use of power, sometimes by people who disingenuously wish to convince us that their abuse of power is really nothing of the sort.

Abuses of Power

One cannot investigate the moral uses of power without considering the all-too-frequent abuses of it. The reasons people abuse their power are not at all difficult to discern. In most instances, the cause is simply selfishness or greed. Some people may find power intoxicating, especially if they have a history of feeling powerless and can compensate for this by imposing their will on others. (The classic school-yard bully may be a case in point.) In the relatively few cases of genuine sadism, people may find it perversely pleasurable to inflict pain on others. But, on the whole, abuses of power result from the desire of some to further their own interests at the expense of others; such abuses are especially prevalent in situations where it is easy or convenient to ignore the rights of others.

The more subtle question of moral psychology concerns the way in which the possession of power may itself be corrosive. The maxim "Power corrupts" may be wrong as a historical generalization, but a more plausible substitute might be "Those with power frequently (inevitably?) feel tempted to abuse it" or even "Power tends to blind those who possess it to their own susceptibility to abuse it." There can be little doubt that there is something seductive about power; and the greater or more unusual the power, the more seductive it can become. If the power to prescribe drugs or grade tests is sometimes subject to abuse, the power to control vast sums of money or to command armies and change the course of history is still more so.

What is it about power that so readily blinds us to the moral constraints that attend its use? What makes power corrupting, or at least potentially so?

At least one answer lies in the fact that moral principles are always "other regarding," as many ethicists have put it. That is, being moral is primarily a matter of respecting the rights, needs, and desires of others, whether those "others" are in our immediate circle of friends or people halfway around the world whom we will never meet. But to have power, as we noted, is always to have the freedom to act on our own desires and needs and especially to impose our will on others. It follows, then, that having power by its very nature carries with it the potential to run roughshod over the rights and needs of others in the course of pursuing the satisfaction of our own desires. Because the exercise of power is a means to get or do what *I* want, it tempts me to put myself ahead of others and to forget that their rights and needs are as precious and unalienable as my own.

Preventing Abuses of Power

It is one thing, of course, to recognize the seductiveness of power and quite another to curb it. What general principles can we adduce to help us ensure that our use of power is moral? What values can we appeal to as guides to the exercise of power? The list that follows is by no means exhaustive, but it gives us, at least, a point of departure.

First and foremost, the use of power must always be constrained to some extent by a moral principle, whether that is respect for the rights of others, the goal of creating a just society, or the cultivation of certain moral virtues. In certain cases, we have the power to deprive others of their freedoms or to force them to do things against their will, as when the police arrest someone suspected of committing a crime. But even individuals in police custody have a right to remain silent; certainly they have a right to be free of physical coercion or torture. To suggest otherwise is not only to trample on individual rights but also to make a mockery of justice. The use of power, then, is morally justifiable only when it does not unduly deprive others of what is owed to them, especially of the rights most closely connected to their personhood or their human dignity.

The moral exercise of power also relies on clear principles that apply equally to everyone. Whenever someone claims that she has a unique right to use her power in ways that would be illegitimate if someone else did so, we have strong reason to suspect abuse of power. The principle of American democracy that "we are a government of laws, not of men" is meant to capture precisely this point. The moral legitimacy of power derives from principles or laws that are impartial. Like the famed symbol of the blindfolded woman holding the scales of justice, the use of power cannot be just if it is idiosyncratic or tailored to serve the needs of some at the expense of others.

Power is most likely to be used morally if it is balanced by other powers that constrain its use. Again, we see a classic example of this in the composition of our federal government, in which executive, legislative, and judicial powers are carefully and explicitly designed to keep one another in check. Power unchecked, no matter who wields it, readily lends itself to abuse, for all the reasons we have enumerated.

Accountability and transparency are critical tools for curbing the abuse of power. Most people, even if they are not committed to doing what is moral, are at least committed to *appearing* to be moral. People who engage in fraud, assault, cheating, and all manner of other abuses of power generally act as they do because they believe that they can get away with it. When there are effective mechanisms in place to scrutinize those who have power, the risk that they will abuse that power is greatly reduced.

The same principle applies to what we might call "internal accountability," or the exercise of conscience. People who have power—which is to say, all of us—need to be self-reflective about the ways in which we use that power. This is not only a matter of paying attention to our conscience at the moment when we are tempted to abuse our power. It is also about cultivating the habit of self-awareness, noticing the situations in which we are most prone to promoting ourselves at the expense of others, and being aware of our own moral blind spots, as it were. In this way we can nurture the sorts of internal constraints that will minimize the likelihood of unconsciously abusing our power.

It is important to remember throughout this discussion that it is not only the exercise of power that can be morally problematic; frequently, the failure to use one's power can be immoral as well. There are sins of omission as well as sins of commission. Glaring examples of this in the political sphere involve the failure to intervene in cases of genocide or famine, when the fate of millions of innocent victims can rest in the hands of those who live far removed from the tragedy. But there are far less dramatic instances in which the failure to act is morally indefensible: if we do not speak out in defense of those who have been discriminated against, if we fail to help those in our own society who lack basic social services, if we fail to blow the whistle on those who abuse their power in the workplace—in short, anytime we acquiesce to injustice we have failed to perform our moral duty. These are situations in which we may have more power to affect a situation than we realize, and it often takes a courageous individual to call us to action. But failure to appreciate the extent of our power does not exonerate us. In the words of Edmund Burke, "All that is necessary for evil to succeed is that good men do nothing."

Jewish Insights on Power

What lessons shall we derive from this exploration of the ethics of power? More specifically, what values about the use of power will we find in the Jewish tradition? Surely Judaism does not counsel us to avoid the use of power altogether, for that is impossible. Nor does Judaism teach us to avoid the pursuit of more than a bare minimum of power, for it is partly through maintaining a balance of power that we help prevent too much power from accumulating in the hands of a few unscrupulous people. How, then, shall we proceed?

A first clue might be found in two contrasting passages attributed to the early Rabbis:

> Rabban Gamliel taught: Be wary of the authorities. They do not befriend anyone unless it is serves their own needs. They appear as a friend when it is to their advantage, but do not stand by a person in his hour of need (Avot 2:3).

> Rabbi Hananiah, the Deputy High Priest, taught: Pray for the welfare of the government, for if people did not fear it, they would swallow each other alive (Avot 3:2).

Taken together, these two passages illustrate the importance both of respecting and of questioning the powerful. Political power can be a source of social stability and a check on the self-interest of individuals who would take advantage of others if given the opportunity to do so. And the same power can itself become a vehicle for promoting self-interest, for behaving in a way that ignores the needs of others. The use of power is necessary and good, but also dangerous and potentially immoral. These are the guideposts that our tradition provides us for navigating our way toward a balanced understanding of power.

We could make a similar point in relation to the two landmark events of modern Jewish history: the Holocaust and the creation of a politically independent state in Israel. The Holocaust surely stands as a grim reminder of the perils for Jews of powerlessness. When we focus our gaze on this immense tragedy, we know that we must "never again" permit others to control our fate, trample our rights, or deny our humanity. The modern state of Israel, by contrast, is an example of the promise, but also of the peril, of exercising power. With political power comes national self-determination but also the potential to abuse that power in relation to minorities, whether these are Sephardic Jews at the hands of Ashkenazim or Israeli Arabs at the hands of Israeli Jews or Palestinians at the hands of Israelis. Here, again, power is both necessary and potentially open to misuse.

We live in a world in which the concentration of power is increasing dramatically—the power of large corporations to control the marketplace; the power of the United States, as the world's sole superpower, to control geopolitical events; the power of the wealthy to accumulate an ever greater proportion of the resources in our country; the power of technology and those who develop and market it to control the quality of our lives; and the power of ideas, which now travel electronically around the world with the push of a button, to move people to action. In all these ways and many others, our lives are subject to powerful people who cannot easily be held accountable. This requires us to consider anew the cautionary note sounded centuries ago about being wary of those in power.

It is no less true that in a world of competing interests, materialism, and radical individualism, we as individuals must be vigilant about exercising the power we have, especially the power to challenge others when they abuse their power. This means that we will need to continually reinforce our determination not to abdicate our responsibilities, which includes recognizing the power we have to make a difference. We may not escape into indifference or passivity, lest we unwittingly become accomplices to those who would be only too happy to abuse their power.

In the end, there is no escaping power or the responsibility that inevitably accompanies it. In this sense, our exercise of power—whether in our most intimate personal relationships or in the political struggles between nations—will ultimately be judged by the extent to which we wield it justly, humanely, and with humility. This is undoubtedly what the Torah has in mind when it requires that the Israelite king keep a copy of the Torah close at hand.

> When he is seated in his royal throne, he shall have a copy of this Teaching written for him on a scroll by the levitical priests. Let it remain with him and let him read in it all his life, so that he may learn to revere the Lord his God, to observe faithfully every word of this Teaching as well as these laws. Thus he will not act haughtily toward his fellows or deviate from the Instruction to the right or to the left, to the end that he and his descendants may reign long in the midst of Israel. (Deuteronomy 17:18–20)

From this perspective, all earthly power, even the power of the king, is really just a gift, perhaps even a sacred trust. We have a right to that power only insofar as we use it in accord with God's will, as expressed in Torah. And what applies to the king applies also to the teacher, the parent, the rabbi, the political leader, the professional, the CEO—to all of us who presume to wield power over others. Our goal should be neither to have more power nor less, but only to use our power as a channel for God's power, which the tradition describes as that which "is good and bestows goodness."

Glossary

adamah Ground.

Ashkenazic From the Hebrew word referring to Germany, the name given to Jews of central European descent and to the religious-cultural practices of those Jews. Ashkenazic Jews are often contrasted with Sephardic Jews and their traditions, deriving from Spain and North Africa.

Beth Hatfutsoth "Museum of the Diaspora," which houses important exhibits tracing Jewish religious, cultural, and communal life throughout the world, located on the campus of Tel Aviv University in Israel.

brit milah Circumcision. Traditionally performed on baby boy on the eighth day after his birth. See Genesis 17.

Chabad Another name for the Lubavitch sect of Hasidic Jews, founded by Rabbi Shneur Zalman of Liadi in the late eighteenth century in Russia. The name "chabad" is based on a Hebrew acronym for the words "wisdom, understanding, knowledge."

chai Life.

challah/challot The special twisted egg bread traditionally made for the Sabbath and other Jewish holidays.

Day of Atonement (Heb., Yom Kippur) The holiest day of the Jewish calendar, which falls on the 10th day of the Hebrew month of Tishrei, devoted to fasting and penitential prayers.

Devarim (Deuteronomy), the fifth book of the Torah.

dina d'malkhuta dina "The law of the land is the law." The talmudic rule that Jews are subject to the legal authority of the non-Jewish societies in which they live (Babylonian Talmud, Nedarim 28a; Gittin 10b; Bava Kamma 113a; Bava Batra 54b–55a).

dover emet bilvavo "Speaking honestly in one's heart" (lit.). Being honest with oneself.

dugma ishit "a personal example," that is, serving as a personal example of Jewish values.

Ehyeh asher ehyeh "I Am-Was-Will Be Who/What I Am-Was-Will Be." The explanation God offers to Moses of God's name, meant to emphasize the impenetrable mystery of God's nature, or perhaps God's transcending of time or causality. See Exodus 3:14.

goy/goyim "Nation(s), non-Jew(s)" (lit.). Sometimes used with derogatory connotations.

halakhah Jewish law.

Hasidim "pious ones," adherents of a religious movement that began in Europe in the late 18th century and traces its origins to the teachings of Israel Baal Shem Tov, who, in turn, had popularized many earlier mystical teachings in Judaism. Hasidism emphasizes ecstatic worship, cleaving to God, and joy in the performance of the commandments. Dozens of different sects of Hasidim evolved as individual teachers adapted these teachings, many of which continue to the present.

Havdalah "Separation" (lit.). The ceremony that separates the Sabbath from the rest of the week.

hesed "Lovingkindness" (lit.). One of the qualities of God and one of the virtues that Jews aspire to emulate.

hevruta "Partner" (lit.). In traditional Jewish text study, students work in pairs.

hiddur mitzvah "Beautification of a commandment" (lit.). A traditional concept that a biblical commandment should be performed in a way that is aesthetically pleasing and uplifting, rather than perfunctory.

Hillel One of the pre-eminent Rabbinic sages in the first century B.C.E. who was revered by subsequent generations of rabbis and whose teachings helped shape early Rabbinic Judaism. His teachings were frequently juxtaposed with those of another scholar of the time, Shammai. Also, the name of contemporary Jewish student centers on college campuses, named for the great sage.

Jewish Federation The central organization in each Jewish community that annually raises funds and distributes them to Jewish institutions both within the local community and in countries around the world.

kashrut Kosher. The dietary rules prescribed by the Torah and observed by traditional Jews. See, for example, Leviticus 11 and Deuteronomy 14 "Glatt (lit., Smooth) Kosher" refers to an especially stringent standard for Kosher meat used by some Orthodox Jews.

kavanah Intention. A concept with wide-ranging application in Jewish law, especially in relation to prayer, the proper performance of a ritual act, or matters of liability in civil and criminal affairs.

kavod Honor. Frequently used in connection with the honor due one's parents or, more generally, of honoring God's creatures.

kiddush "Sanctification" (lit). The prayer said over a cup of wine at the evening and noon meals of Sabbaths and holidays.

klei kodesh Holy instruments (or holy articles); singular, *kli kodesh*. Sometimes used metaphorically for rabbis, cantors, and Jewish educators.

koach Force, power.

kol Yisrael arevim ze le ze "All Jews are responsible for one another" (Babylonian Talmud, Shevu'ot 39a). This talumdic phrase reflects the strong traditional values of Jews' interdependence and their collective responsibility.

kup "Head" (lit., Yiddish). Used figuratively as well as literally, as in "He has a good *kup* for Talmud study."

lifnim meshurat hadin Supererogation. Doing more than the law requires (or pressing one's legal claims less than the law permits).

lo tishkach "Never forget." See Deuteronomy 25: 17–19.

Maccabees A group of Jewish zealots in Palestine who led a revolt against the Syrians in 168 B.C.E. The holiday of Hanukkah celebrates their victory.

Maimonides, Moses (1135–1204) Enormously influential Jewish philosopher, legalist, and physician in Spain and North Africa.

malach/malachim "Messenger(s)." Human or divine.

mechitzah A partition separating men and women in Orthodox synagogues.

mensch/menschlichkeit "Man/humanity" (lit., Yiddish). Refers to the popular traditional concept of human decency; one who is morally honorable and sensitive to the needs of others is said to be a mensch.

middat ha-din The attribute of strict justice. One of God's two main attributes in relationship with humankind.

middat ha-rachamim The attribute of mercy or compassion. The other of God's two main attributes.

mikveh Ritual bath. Used by women for purification after the conclusion of their menstrual periods before reestablishing sexual relations with their husbands, also as part of the ritual for conversion to Judaism and in other instances of ritual or spiritual purification. See Leviticus 15 and Numbers 19.

minyan "Quorum" (lit.). The 10 adults (traditionally, 10 men) required to constitute a quorum for purposes of public prayer.

Mi She Berakh A prayer for healing named for the first three words of the traditional Hebrew text, "May the one who blessed . . . [our ancestors . . . bless those who are ill . . .]."

mishkan "Dwelling place" (lit.). The name of the ancient Tabernacle that the Isarelites carried with them during their wanderings in the desert. The Tabernacle, and later the permanent Temple in Jerusalem, were understood as the place where God's presence dwelled on earth.

Mishnah "Teaching" (lit.). The name of the Hebrew law code written in Palestine in circa 200 C.E., traditionally ascribed to Rabbi Judah the Prince. The Mishnah greatly expands on biblical law and later becomes the foundation of the Talmud.

mitzvah/mitzvot "Commandment(s)." According to tradition, there were 613 divinely ordained mitzvot in the Torah, and the Rabbis added many more based on the Oral tradition.

mohel Ritual circumciser.

nigun "Melody" (lit.). One of the haunting wordless melodies sung by Hasidic Jews.

ona'ah "Coercion" (lit.). Unfair exploitation through over-charging

oz "power."

parashah Torah portion. The set reading from the Pentateuch for a given Sabbath or holiday, usually encompassing several chapters.

Rebbe A rabbi and spiritual leader of an Hasidic community.

Rosh Hodesh The new moon, which marks the beginning of the new month on the Hebrew calendar. Some contemporary Jewish women have created ceremonies to celebrate Rosh Hodesh.

ruach Spirit.

Selichot Petitions for forgiveness.

Sh'ma The central prayer text of Judaism, affirming the oneness and uniqueness of God and the commandment to love God and observe God's commandments (Deuteronomy 6:4–9).

shtetl One of the small, predominantly Jewish villages of eastern Europe from which many Jews emigrated to America or Israel.

shtetl bubbes Jewish grandmothers.

Shulchan Arukh "The set table." The name of the classic code of Jewish law composed by Rabbi Yosef Karo (1488–1575) and completed in 1565.

teshuvah "An answer." A rabbinic ruling in response to a question in Jewish law. Also "turning" or "response" (lit.); repentance: one of the key moral concepts in Jewish life.

tikun olam "Repair of the world" (lit.). The idea, central to Jewish tradition, that it is the task of humankind to complete the process of creation that God began. The concept takes on special cosmological significance in the work of the Kabbalists, or Jewish mystics.

tikvah Hope.

tokhehah "Obligation to reprove [those who transgress]." See Leviticus 19:17.

Tu b'Shevat "15th of [Hebrew month of] Shevat," a minor holiday referred to as the New Year for trees. Falling in the spring, it marks the beginning of the new growing season for fruit-bearing trees.

tzeniut "Modesty" (lit.). Used most often in connection with the traditional value that people should dress in a way that is not revealing or sexually provocative.

yetzer ha-rah "Evil inclination" (lit.). That aspect of human nature that prompts us to sin.

zachor Remember.

Suggestions for Further Reading

General Sources on Jewish Ethics

Abramowitz, Yosef I., and Susan Silverman. *Jewish Family & Life: Traditions, Holidays, and Values for Today's Parents and Children.* New York: Golden Books, 1997.

Agus, Jacob B. *The Vision and the Way: An Interpretation of Jewish Ethics.* New York: Frederick Ungar, 1966.

Alpert, Rebecca T., and Jacob J. Staub. *Exploring Judaism: A Reconstructionist Approach.* Expanded and updated. Jenkintown, Pa.: Jewish Reconstructionist Federation, 2000.

Amsel, Nachum. *The Jewish Encyclopedia of Moral and Ethical Issues.* Northvale, N.J.: Jason Aronson, 1994.

Birnbaum, Philip. *Encyclopedia of Jewish Concepts.* New York: Hebrew Publishing Company, 1964, 1995.

Borowitz, Eugene B. *Exploring Jewish Ethics: Papers on Covenant Responsibility.* Detroit, Mich.: Wayne State University Press, 1990.

_____, ed. *Reform Jewish Ethics and the Halakhah.* West Orange, N.J.: Behrman House, 1994.

Borowitz, Eugene B., and Frances Weinman Schwartz. *The Jewish Moral Virtues.* Philadelphia: The Jewish Publication Society, 1999.

Breslauer, S. Daniel. *A New Jewish Ethics.* New York and Toronto: Edwin Mellon Press, 1983.

Cohen, Jeffery. *Dear Chief Rabbi: From the Correspondence of Chief Rabbi Immanuel Jakobovits on Matters of Jewish Law, Ethics, and Contemporary Issues, 1980–1990.* Hoboken, N.J.: Ktav, 1995.

Cohn, Haim. *Human Rights in Jewish Law.* New York: Ktav and London: Institute of Jewish Affairs, 1984.

Dan, Joseph. *Jewish Mysticism and Jewish Ethics.* Philadelphia: The Jewish Publication Society and Seattle: University of Washington Press, 1986.

Dorff, Elliot N. "The Ethics of Judaism." In *The Blackwell Companion to Judaism.* Ed. Jacob Neusner and Alan J. Avery-Peck, 373–92. Oxford, UK, and Malden, Mass.: Blackwell Publishers, 2000.

_____. *For the Love of God and People: A Philosophy of Jewish Law.* Philadelphia: Jewish Publication Society, 2007, esp. ch. 6.

_____. *Love Your Neighbor and Yourself: A Jewish Approach to Modern Personal Ethics.* Philadelphia: The Jewish Publication Society, 2003.

_____. *Matters of Life and Death: A Jewish Approach to Modern Medical Ethics*. Philadelphia: The Jewish Publication Society, 1998.

_____. *To Do the Right and the Good: A Jewish Approach to Modern Personal Ethics*. Philadelphia: The Jewish Publication Society, 2002.

_____. *The Way into Tikkun Olam (Fixing the World)*. Woodstock, Vt.: Jewish Lights, 2005.

Dorff, Elliot N., and Louis E. Newman, eds. *Contemporary Jewish Ethics and Morality: A Reader*. New York: Oxford University Press, 1995.

Dorff, Elliot N., and Arthur Rosett. *A Living Tree: The Roots and Growth of Jewish Law*. Albany: State University of New York Press, 1988. See esp. 110–23; 249–57.

Dresner, Samuel H., and Byron L. Sherwin. *Judaism: The Way of Sanctification*. New York: United Synagogue of America, 1978.

Fox, Marvin, ed. *Modern Jewish Ethics: Theory and Practice*. Columbus: Ohio State University Press, 1975.

Freund, Richard A. *Understanding Jewish Ethics*. 2 vols. San Francisco: EMText and Lewiston, N.Y.: Edwin Mellon Press, 1990.

Goldman, Alex J. *Judaism Confronts Contemporary Issues*. New York: Shengold Publishers, 1978.

Goldstein, Niles E., and Steven S. Mason. *Judaism and Spiritual Ethics*. New York: Union of American Hebrew Congregations Press, 1996.

Goodman, Lenn E. *Judaism, Human Rights, and Human Values*. New York: Oxford University Press, 1998.

Gordis, Robert. *The Dynamics of Judaism: A Study in Jewish Law*. Bloomington: Indiana University Press, 1990.

_____. *Judaic Ethics for a Lawless World*. New York: Jewish Theological Seminary of America, 1986.

Jacobs, Louis. *Jewish Personal and Social Ethics*. West Orange, N.J.: Behrman House, 1990.

Kadushin, Max. *Worship and Ethics: A Study in Rabbinic Judaism*. Evanston, Ill.: Northwestern University Press, 1964.

Kaplan, Mordecai M. *The Future of the American Jew*. New York: Reconstructionist Press, 1948, 1967. [Chap. 15 was reprinted as a separate book: *Basic Values in Jewish Religion*. New York: Reconstuctionist Press, 1957.]

Kellner, Menachem Marc, ed. *Contemporary Jewish Ethics*. New York: Sanhedrin Press, 1978.

Klagsbrun, Francine. *Voices of Wisdom: Jewish Ideas and Ethics for Everyday Living*. New York: Pantheon Books and Philadelphia: The Jewish Publication Society, 1980.

Malsin, Simeon J., ed. *Gates of Mitzvah—Shaarei Mitzvah*. New York: Central Conference of American Rabbis Press, 1986.

Meir, Asher. *The Jewish Ethicist: Everyday Ethics for Business and Life*. Jersey City, N.J.: Ktav and Jerusalem: Business Ethics Center of Jerusalem, 2005.

Newman, Louis E. *An Introduction to Jewish Ethics*. Upper Saddle River, N.J.: Pearson Prentice Hall, 2005.

_____. *Past Imperatives: Studies in the History and Theory of Jewish Ethics*. Albany: State University of New York Press, 1998.

Novak, David. *Jewish Social Ethics*. New York: Oxford University Press, 1992.

Olitzky, Kerry M., and Rachel T. Sabath. *Striving toward Virtue: A Contemporary Guide for Jewish Ethical Behavior*. Hoboken, N.J.: Ktav, 1996.

Sacks, Jonathan. *To Heal a Fractured World: The Ethics of Responsibility*. New York: Schocken Books, 2005.

Schwarz, Sidney. *Judaism and Justice: The Jewish Passion to Repair the World*. Woodstock, Vt.: Jewish Lights, 2006.

Shatz, David, Chaim I. Waxman, and Nathan J. Diament, eds. *Tikkun Olam: Social Responsibility in Jewish Thought and Law*. Northvale, N.J.: Jason Aronson, 1997.

Sherwin, Byron L. *Jewish Ethics for the Twenty-First Century: Living in the Image of God*. Syracuse, N.Y.: Syracuse University Press, 2000.

Sherwin, Byron L., and Seymour J. Cohen. *Creating An Ethical Jewish Life: A Practical Introduction to Classic Teachings on How to Be a Jew*. Woodstock, Vt.: Jewish Lights, 2001.

_____. *How to Be a Jew: Ethical Teachings of Judaism*. Northvale, N.J.: Jason Aronson, 1992.

Siegel, Richard, Michael Strassfield, and Sharon Strassfield, eds. *The Jewish Catalogue*. Philadelphia: The Jewish Publication Society of America, 1973.

Stone, Ira. *A Responsible Life: The Spiritual Path of Mussar*. New York: Aviv Press (Rabbinical Assembly), 2006.

Telushkin, Joseph. *A Code of Jewish Ethics*. Volume I: *You Shall Be Holy*. New York: Bell Tower (a division of Crown Publishing, Random House), 2006.

_____. *Jewish Wisdom: Ethical, Spiritual, and Historical Lessons from the Great Works and Thinkers*. New York: William Morrow & Co., 1994.

Vorspan, Albert, and David Saperstein. *Tough Choices: Jewish Perspectives on Social Justice.* New York: Union of American Hebrew Congregations Press, 1992.

Washofsky, Mark. *Jewish Living: A Guide to Contemporary Reform Practice.* New York: Union of American Hebrew Congregations, 2001.

Wurzburger, Walter S. *Ethics of Responsibility: Pluralistic Approaches to Covenantal Ethics.* Philadelphia: The Jewish Publication Society, 1994.

Jewish Sources on Ethical Issues Concerning Power

Alford, C. Fred. "Whistleblowers and the Narrative of Ethics." *Journal of Social Philosophy* 32, no. 4 (winter 2001), 402–18.

Bleich, J. David. "Caterers' Claim for Cancellation of Wedding." In his *Contemporary Halakhic Problems.* Vol. 4. New York: Ktav and Yeshiva University Press, 1995, 367–70.

_____. "Organized Labor." In his *Contemporary Halakhic Problems.* Vol. 1. New York: Ktav and Yeshiva University Press, 1977, 186–89.

_____. "Physicians' Fees." In his *Contemporary Halakhic Problems.* Vol. 2. New York: Ktav and Yeshiva University Press, 1983, 68–74.

_____. "Physicians' Strikes." In his *Contemporary Halakhic Problems.* Vol. 3. New York: Ktav and Yeshiva University Press, 1989, 18–25.

_____. "Rabbinic Contracts." In his *Contemporary Halakhic Problems.* Vol. 1. New York: Ktav and Yeshiva University Press, 1977, 71–73.

_____. "Severance Pay." In his *Contemporary Halakhic Problems.* Vol. 2. New York: Ktav Publishing House and Yeshiva University Press, 1983, 111–13.

_____. "Teachers' Claims for Lost Wages" In his *Contemporary Halakhic Problems.* Vol. 4. New York: Ktav and Yeshiva University Press, 1995, 364–67.

_____. "Teachers' Unions." In his *Contemporary Halakhic Problems.* Vol. 2. New York: Ktav and Yeshiva University Press, 1983, 132–34.

_____. "Tenure." In his *Contemporary Halakhic Problems.* Vol. 1. New York: Ktav and Yeshiva University Press, 1977, 189–94.

Cohen, Seymour. "Judaism and the Worlds of Business and Labor." *Proceedings of the Rabbinical Assembly* 25 (1961), 17–44.

Dorff, Elliot N. *To Do the Right and the Good: A Jewish Approach to Modern Social Ethics.* Philadelphia: The Jewish Publication Society, 2002, esp. ch. 4, "The King's Torah: Judaism and National Policy," and ch. 8, "Communal Forgiveness."

Fendel, Zechariah. *The Halacha and Beyond: Providing an Insight into the Fiscal Ethical Responsibilities of the Torah Jew.* New York: Hashkafah Publications, 1983.

Frank, Daniel H. *Autonomy and Judaism: The Individual and the Community in Jewish Philosophical Thought.* Albany: State University of New York Press, 1992.

Freeman, Gordon M. *The Heavenly Kingdom: Aspects of Political Thought in the Talmud and Midrash.* Lanham, Md.: University Press of America, 1986.

Golinkin, David. "The Basic Principles of Jewish Business Ethics." *Insight Israel* 3, no. 1 (October 2002). (Published by The Schechter Institute of Jewish Studies in Jerusalem.)

Greenberg, Irving. "The Ethics of Jewish Power." In *Contemporary Jewish Ethics and Morality.* Ed. Elliot N. Dorff and Louis E. Newman. New York: Oxford University Press, 1995, 403–21.

Herring, Basil. *Jewish Ethics and Halakhah for Our Time.* Vol. II. Hoboken, N.J.: Ktav and New York: Yeshiva University Press, 1989. See esp. "Truth and Deception in the Marketplace," 221–79.

Hirsch, Richard G., *The Way of the Upright: A Jewish View of Economic Justice.* New York: Union of American Hebrew Congregations, 1973. See esp. "Labor—Rights and Responsibilities," 36–62.

Horowitz, George. *The Spirit of Jewish Law.* New York: Central Book Company, 1963. See esp. "Hired Workers," 132–35.

Jacobs, Jill. "Mutual Responsibilities." Available at www.myjewishlearning.com/daily_life/BusinessEthics/BusEthics_in_Practice/J_Ethical_Princpls_in_Busns/Employee_Employer.htm.

Jacobs, Louis. *The Jewish Religion: A Companion.* New York: Oxford University Press, 1995. See esp. "Competition."

Jung, Leo. "The Ethics of Business." In *Contemporary Jewish Ethics.* Ed. Menachem Marc Kellner. New York: Sanhedrin Press, 1978, 332–43.

Jung, Leo, and Aaron Levine. *Business Ethics in Jewish Law.* New York: Hebrew Publishing Company, 1987.

Klein, Isaac. *Responsa and Halakhic Studies.* New York: Ktav, 1975. See esp. chap. 12, "Advertising Practices," and chap. 18, "Business Ethics in the Talmud." (Reprinted Jerusalem: Institute of Applied Halakhah of the Schechter Institute of Jewish Studies, 2005.)

Levine, Aaron. *Case Studies in Jewish Business Ethics.* Hoboken, N.J.: Ktav and New York: Yeshiva University Press, 1999.

Suggestions for Further Reading

_____. *Economic Public Policy and Jewish Law.* Hoboken, N.J.: Ktav and New York: Yeshiva University Press, 1993.

_____. *Economics and Jewish Law.* Hoboken, N.J.: Ktav and New York: Yeshiva University Press, 1987.

_____. *Free Enterprise and Jewish Law: Aspects of Jewish Business Ethics.* Hoboken, N.J.: Ktav and New York: Yeshiva University Press, 1980.

_____. *Moral Issues of the Marketplace in Jewish Law.* Brooklyn, N.Y.: Yashar Books, Inc., 2005.

Levine, Aaron, and Moses L. Pava, eds. *Jewish Business Ethics: The Firm and Its Stakeholders.* Northvale, N.J.: Jason Aronson, 1999.

Luz, Ehud. *Wrestling with an Angel: Power, Morality, and Jewish Identity.* Trans. Michael Swirsky. New Haven, Conn.: Yale University Press, 2003.

Meir, Asher. *The Jewish Ethicist: Everyday Ethics for Business and Life.* Jersey City, N.J.: Ktav and Jerusalem: Business Ethics Center of Jerusalem, 2005.

Mendelsohn, Ezra. *Covenantal Rights: A Study in Jewish Political Theory.* Princeton, N.J.: Princeton University Press, 2000.

_____. *The Jewish Social Contract: An Essay in Political Theology.* Princeton, N.J.: Princeton University Press, 2005.

_____. *On Modern Jewish Politics.* New York: Oxford University Press, 1993.

Mittleman, Alan, Jonathan D. Sarna, and Robert Licht, eds. *Jewish Polity and American Civil Society: Communal Agencies and Religious Movements in the American Public Square.* Lanham, Md.: Rowman & Littlefield, 2002.

_____. *Jews and the American Public Square: Debating Religion and Republic.* Lanham, Md.: Rowman & Littlefield, 2002.

Pava, Moses L. *Business Ethics: A Jewish Perspective.* Jersey City, N.J.: Ktav and New York: Yeshiva University Press, 1997.

Perry, Grant. "The 'Good Jew' Who Went to Jail." *Reform Judaism* 31, no. 2 (winter 2002), 26–31.

Rothenberg, Paula. *Invisible Privilege: A Memoir about Race, Class, and Gender.* Lawrence: University Press of Kansas, 2000.

Rubenstein, W. D. *The Left, the Right and the Jews.* London: Croom Helm, 1982.

Sicker, Martin. *What Judaism Says about Politics: The Political Theology of the Torah.* Northvale, N.J.: Jason Aronson, 1994.

Walzer, Michael, Menachem Lorberbaum, and Noam J. Zohar. *The Jewish Political Tradition.* New Haven, Conn.: Yale University Press, 2000.

Editors and Contributors

Editors

Elliot N. Dorff, rabbi (Jewish Theological Seminary), Ph.D. (Columbia University), is rector and Sol and Anne Dorff Distinguished Professor of Philosophy at the American Jewish University (formerly the University of Judaism) in Los Angeles. Among his 14 books are three award-winning Jewish Publication Society books on Jewish ethics. He and Louis Newman are co-editors of *Contemporary Jewish Ethics and Morality* (1995) and *Contemporary Jewish Theology* (1999). Since 1984 Dorff has served on the Rabbinical Assembly's Committee on Jewish Law and Standards, currently as its chair. He also has served on several federal government advisory commissions dealing with the ethics of health care, sexual responsibility, and research on human subjects; he currently is a member of California's Ethics Committee on embryonic stem cell research.

Louis E. Newman, Ph.D. (Brown University), is the John M. and Elizabeth W. Musser Professor of Religious Studies and director of Judaic Studies at Carleton College. He is the author of *Past Imperatives: Studies in the History and Theory of Jewish Ethics* (1998) and *An Introduction to Jewish Ethics* (2005) as well as co-editor with Elliot Dorff of two anthologies (see above). He is currently working on a book on Jewish views of repentance.

Contributors

Aaron Alexander, rabbi, is currently the Assistant Dean of the Ziegler School of Rabbinic Studies at American Jewish University where he was ordained, earned his master's in rabbinic studies, and currently teaches Practical Halakhah and Codes. Rabbi Alexander received his B.A. in religion from the University of Florida, spent two years studying at the Conservative Yeshiva in Jerusalem, and also spent a year doing graduate work in Talmud and rabbinics at the Jewish Theological Seminary of America.

James S. Diamond, rabbi, teaches in the Program in Judaic Studies at Princeton University. He has written on modern Hebrew literature and Israeli culture. Hillel was the focus of his rabbinical career, and his experience with students and teachers is the primary source of his essay here.

Steven Edelman-Blank, rabbi, received his rabbinic ordination and master's in rabbinic studies from the American Jewish University's Ziegler School of Rabbinic Studies. He holds a B.A. in social studies from Harvard University.

119

Editors and Contributors

Aaron J. Feingold, M.D., is president and senior physician of Raritan Bay Cardiology in Edison, New Jersey. He is a fellow of the American College of Cardiology. He is director of the cardiology division at JFK Medical Center (in Edison) as well as medical director of the Central Jersey Jewish Home for the Aged. He is the current president of The American Friends of Beth Hatefutsoth and a member of the board of trustees of the American Physician Fellowship for Medicine in Israel.

Aaron Feuerstein is the third-generation owner and CEO of Malden Mills in Lawrence, Massachusetts. When the Malden Mills factory burned down in 1995, he continued to pay all his employees their salaries and benefits while the mill was being rebuilt. His devotion to the highest standards of business ethics earned him much notoriety, including a segment on the CBS news magazine *60 Minutes.*

Laura Geller is the senior rabbi of Temple Emanuel in Beverly Hills, California. Before being chosen for this position in 1994, she served as the executive director of the American Jewish Congress, Pacific Southwest Region. She came to AJCongress in 1990 after 14 years as the director of Hillel at the University of Southern California. She has published numerous articles and chapters examining gender issues within Judaism. She graduated from Brown University in 1971 and was ordained by the Hebrew Union College in 1976.

Marc Graboff is president at NBC Universal Television, West Coast, overseeing all business, financial, operational, and administrative matters for NBC Entertainment and NBC Universal Television Studio. He graduated from UCLA in 1977 with a bachelor's degree in communications studies and graduated magna cum laude from Loyola Law School in 1983.

Daniel Held is a teacher and the director of student activities at the Tanenbaum Community Hebrew Academy of Toronto and a graduate student at York University. His experience as an educator bridges the formal and informal in summer programs, youth movements, Hebrew schools, and day schools.

Elizabeth Holtzman is the youngest woman ever elected to the U.S. Congress, where she won national acclaim for her work on the House impeachment panel on President Nixon and for her questioning of President Ford on the Nixon pardon. She was the first member of Congress to uncover Nazi war criminals in the United States and authored the Holtzman Amendment, which facilitates their deportation. She was elected district attorney of Brooklyn (the first woman so elected in New York City) and New York City comptroller (the first woman to hold this position). She practices law in New York City. She is the author of *Who Said It Would Be Easy?* and *The Impeachment of George W. Bush.*

Sandra King was director of Jewish Family Service (JFS) of Los Angeles from 1991 to 2000. She began her history at JFS as a volunteer in 1971, taking time off to earn her master's in social work at UCLA (1973–1975). She returned to JFS, where she worked until her retirement in 2000. She became director of the Frieda Mohr Center for senior services in 1979, director of senior services for JFS in 1981, associate director in 1983, and executive director in 1991.

Gail Labovitz, rabbi, Ph.D., is a professor and chair of the Rabbinics Department at the American Jewish University. She was ordained as a Conservative rabbi by the Jewish Theological Seminary in 1992, where she also earned her Ph.D. in 2002.

Zachary Lazarus was raised in the Midwest and received his B.A. from Wesleyan University in 2006. He majored in religious studies with a focus on Jewish and Israel studies. He now works for the Progressive Jewish Alliance in Los Angeles.

Rachelle Smith is the president of the American Federation of State, County, and Municipal Employees (AFSCME) Local 800.

Henry A. Waxman represents California's 30th Congressional District. In 2007, he became chairman of the Committee on Oversight and Government Reform, the principal investigative committee in the House. From 1997 to 2006, he served as ranking member of the committee, conducting investigations into the high cost of prescription drugs and into the waste, fraud, and abuse in government contracting. He has opposed efforts by the Bush administration to block congressional oversight and roll back health and environmental laws. He has launched investigations of White House ties to Enron, contract abuses in Iraq, and the politicization of science. He holds a bachelor's degree in political science from UCLA and a J.D. degree from the UCLA Law School.

Index

Index